Scripture Prayers Breakthrough

His Will Are Your Answers

Kim Eisnor

Scripture quotations from: King James Version of the Bible; Bible in Basic English; World English Bible

Dictionary references from: Strong's Bible Dictionary; Thayer's Greek Definitions; Webster's Dictionary of American English

Abbreviations superscript & subscripts Reference Chart found at back of book' Superscript & subscripts references are found after the preceding scriptures and names in all the prayers.

Other references from:
John Gill's Exposition of the Entire Bible

www.ScripturePrayer.com
Other Books:
Scripture Prayers
Scripture Devotionals
Scripture Promises

Dedication

This book is dedicated to You my Ishi, the Love of my life who has given me everything from the secret places of Your Chambers. I Love You more than human words can say. My heart dances with beats only for You.

Contents

Acknowledgments

I like to thank the Lord for His continual support and strength, and for the privilege given to pursue this labor of love. I am honored. I also like to thank all the family and friends for their many prayers and support given.

Preface

This book has its roots back to 1998 when I first started to write scripture prayers. I was amazed that I could find topics on everything I was looking for. It took a long time back then to search out the Words of gold. But time well spent, oh how I loved that time. Time with the Lord and His Word was the most precious of all and still is the heartbeat of my life.

It is my prayer that His book will help you see that God will never let you down and is so faithful and cares about all areas of your life. I wrote this book because He asked me to and I am in Love with the One Who inspired it to be penned so long ago. He is my inspiration, my direction, my hope, my Love, my Ishi.

And it is because of this I was led to make these prayers personal to Him from You. And asked the Lord "Are You Sure about this?" The answer I received was a scripture beckoning yes !

Deuteronomy 32:3(KJV) Because I will publish(H7121)the Name of the Lord(H3068): ascribe the greatness unto our God.(H430)

The References to this scripture "Call out to and properly address by Name"H7121 "the Self Existent Eternal Jehovah" H3068 "Eloheem" H430

So here is Deuteronomy 32:3(KJV) written with the definitions. "Because I will Call out to and properly address by Name, the Name of the Self Existent Eternal Jehovah: ascribe the greatness unto our Eloheem."

Introduction

Do you find yourself wanting to know if your prayers will be answered? Well praying the scriptures of God's Word guarantees you will receive answers because God's integrity is unmatched and He does what He says. Want proof as to why pray the Word of God. It is written in Isaiah 55:11*(KJV)* So shall my word be that goes forth out of my mouth: it shall not return unto me void, but it shall accomplish that which I please, and it shall prosper in the thing whereto I sent it.

Imagine that, God actually accomplishes what is spoken and it prospers! Hmmm I wonder if we saw what our words prospered in and saw what they did, if we would change what we say. But that's a topic for a whole other book.

You will also discover some of the many treasure truths of gold that

God has given to us and that He promises to fulfill.

2 Corinthians 1:20*(KJV)* For all the promises of God in Him are yea, and in Him Amen, unto the glory of God by us.

There are thousands of promises waiting to be prayed, preparing to be birthed. And some of those promises are just what you have been looking for.

I know many of us have had broken promises, but God does not lie. It is written in Numbers 23:19*(KJV)* God is not a man, that he should lie; neither the son of man, that he should repent: hath he said, and shall he not do it? or hath he spoken, and shall he not make it good? He does what He says and you can count on Him and His Word. Aren't you getting excited to experience breakthrough prayers? But wait, there is more.

Did you know that the angels listen for His Word to be Spoken and then they act on it. It is written in Ps

103:20[KJV] *Bless the LORD, ye his angels, that excel in strength, that do his commandments, hearkening unto the voice of his Word.* I like the fact that praying the Word of God releases angels into action, and the ones assigned to me have lots to keep them busy.

We are told to pray the will of God. It is written in Matthew 6:10[KJV] *Thy kingdom come. Thy will be done in earth, as it is in heaven.*

Pray according to His will *And this is the confidence that we have in him, that, if we ask any thing according to his will, he heareth us:* 1 John 5:14[KJV]. *And if we know that he hear us, whatsoever we ask, we know that we have the petitions that we desired of him.* 1 John 5:15[KJV].

His Word is settled in Heaven. It is written in Ps 119:89[KJV] *Forever, O LORD, thy Word is settled in heaven.* With all the confusion in the world it is a blessing to know that God's Word is settled, there is no confusion in that.

*It is written in Hebrews 11:3[(KJV)]
Through faith we understand that
the worlds were framed by the Word
of God, so that things which are seen
were not made of things which do
appear. God framed everything with
and by His Word.*

*It is written in Galatians 3:26[(KJV)]
For ye are all the children of God by
faith in Christ Jesus. Since we are
His Children we can act like our
heavenly Father.*

*I pray this first collection of His
prayers will inspire you and wrap
you in the Love for His Word as only
He can. I pray that the breath of the
Almighty would breathe afresh and
visit you in the prayers of this book.*

Acceptable Speech

Heavenly Father set a watch, O Self Existent Eternal Jehovah[a], before my mouth; keep the door of my lips.[1] Keep my tongue from evil, and my lips from speaking guile.[2] Let me keep a watch on my mouth and keep my life; let me not be like those whose lips are open wide and have destruction.[3] The wicked is snared by the transgression of his lips: but the just shall come out of trouble.[4] Let me be like the just that comes out of trouble.

Where there is much talk there will be no end to sin, but he who keeps his mouth shut does wisely.[5] Please give me wisdom to shut my mouth. Wherefore, me a beloved brethren, let me be swift to hear, slow to speak, slow to wrath.[6] Let me be like one who keeps watch over my mouth and my tongue and keeps my soul from troubles.[7] Let no corrupt communication proceed out of my mouth, but that which is good to the use of edifying, that it may minister grace unto the hearers.[8] Neither filthiness, nor foolish talking, nor jesting, which are not convenient: but rather giving of thanks.[9]

For my mouth shall speak truth; and wickedness is an abomination to my lips.[10] Let my speech be always with grace, seasoned with salt, that I may know how I ought to answer every man.[11] For it is said, Let me a person who has a love of life, desiring to see good days, keep my tongue from evil and my lips from words of deceit:[12]

And let me be turned from evil and do good; searching for peace and going after it with all my heart.[13] For the eyes of You Kurios the Master[b] are on the upright, and Your ears are open to my prayers: but the face of You Kurios the Master[c] are against those who do evil.[14] *Let my mouth be filled with Your praise and with Your honor all the day.*[15] *I cover and seal this prayer with the Blood of Jesus. In His Name Amen*

Scripture References

1. Ps 141:3 KJV
2. Ps 34:13 KJV
3. Prov 13:3 BBE
4. Prov 12:13 KJV
5. Prov 10:19 BBE
6. Jas 1:19 KJV
7. Prov 21:23 BBE
8. Eph 4:29 KJV
9. Eph 5:4 KJV
10. Prov 8:7 KJV
11. Col 4:6 KJV
12. 1Pet 3:10 BBE
13. 1Pet 3:11 BBE
14. 1Pet 3:12 BBE
15. Ps 71:8 KJV

Strong's and Thayer's References

a. Ps 141:3 H3068
b. 1Pet 3:12 G2962
c. 1Pet 3:12 G2962

3

Against Deception

Abba I am living in a strange land: do not let your teachings be kept secret from me.[1] I am full of hate and disgust for false words; but I am a lover of Your law.[2] For this reason I have greater love for Your teachings than for gold, even for shining gold.[3] Because of it I keep straight in all things by Your orders; and I am a hater of every false way.[4]

Through Your precepts, I get understanding; therefore I hate every false way.[5] Let me not put hope in what is false, falling into error: for I do not want to get deceit as my reward.[6] For if I think myself to be something, when I am nothing, I deceive myself.[7]

Keep me from malice that may be concealed by deception, but let wickedness be exposed in the assembly.[8] Don't let me be deceived!

And keep me from evil companionships that corrupt good morals.⁹ Let me take heed, that my heart be not deceived, and turn aside, and serve other gods, and worship them;¹⁰ Keep me from evil men and impostors who will grow worse and worse, deceiving and being deceived.¹¹ Let no man beguile me of my reward in a voluntary humility and worshipping of angels, intruding into those things which he has not seen, vainly puffed up by his fleshly mind.¹² It is written if anyone, or an angel from heaven, preach any other gospel unto me than the truth, let him be accursed.¹³

And as Jesus answered and said unto them, Take heed that no man deceive you.¹⁴ For many shall come in my name, saying, I am Christ the Anointed Messiahª; and shall deceive many.¹⁵ For there shall arise false Christs, and false prophets, and shall show great signs and wonders;

insomuch that, if it were possible, they shall deceive the very elect.[16]

I am asking You to keep me from deception from false Christs and false prophets. Let me not be a worshipper of false gods and give up my only hope.[17] If I say that I have no sin, I deceive myself, and the truth is not in me.[18] If I confess my sins, You are faithful and just to forgive me my sins, and to cleanse me from all unrighteousness.[19] I have chosen the way of truth. I have set your ordinances before me.[20] I cover and seal this prayer with the Blood of Jesus. In His Name Amen.

Scripture References

1. Ps 119:19 BBE
2. Ps 119:163 BBE
3. Ps 119:127 BBE
4. Ps 119:128 BBE
5. Ps 119:104 WEB
6. Job 15:31 BBE
7. Gal 6:3 KJV
8. Prov 26:26 WEB
9. 1Cor 15:33 WEB
10. Deut 11:16 KJV
11. 2Tim 3:13 WEB
12. Col 2:18 KJV
13. Gal 1:8 KJV
14. Matt 24:4 KJV
15. Matt 24:5 KJV
16. Matt 24:24 KJV
17. Jonah 2:8 BBE
18. 1John 1:8 KJV
19. 1John 1:9 KJV
20. Ps119:30 WEB

Strong's and Thayer's References

a. Matt 24:5 G5547

Assurance of Salvation

Abba it is written that this is the record, that You Theos the Godhead Trinity[a] has given to me eternal life, and this life is in Your Son.[1] I that has the Son has life; and he that has not the Son of Theos the Godhead Trinity[b] has not life.[2] These things have been written unto me that believe on the name of the Son of Theos the Godhead Trinity[c]; that I may know that I have eternal life, and that I may believe on the name of the Son of Theos the Godhead Trinity[d].[3]

Hereby I know that I dwell in Him, and He in me, because He has given me of His Spirit.[4] The Spirit itself bears witness with my spirit, that I am a child of Your's Theos the Godhead Trinity[e].[5] But since I received You, You gave me power to become a child of Your's Theos the Godhead Trinity[f], even to me that believes on Your name.[6] For since I am led by the Spirit of You Theos the Godhead Trinity[g], I am a child of Your's Theos the Godhead Trinity[h].[7] For I have not received the spirit of bondage again to fear; but I have received the Spirit of adoption, whereby I cry, Abba, Father.[8] The Spirit itself bears witness with my spirit, that I am a child of Your's Theos the Godhead Trinity[i].[9] And if a child, then an heir; heir of Your's Theos the Godhead Trinity[j], and a joint-heir with Christ; if so be that I suffer with him, that I may be also glorified together.[10]

That You Christ may dwell in my heart by faith; that being rooted and grounded in love,[11] Not by works of righteousness which I have done, but according to Your mercy You saved me, by the washing of regeneration, and renewing of the Holy Ghost;[12] For by grace I am saved through faith; and that not of myself: it is the gift of You Theos the Godhead Trinity[k]:[13] Not of works, lest I should boast.[14] Therefore being justified by faith, I have peace with You Theos the Godhead Trinity[l] through my Kurios the Master[m] Jesus the anointed Messiah[n]:[15] For I am born of You Theos the Godhead Trinity[o] and overcome the world: and this is the victory that overcomes the world, even my faith.[16] Being confident of this very thing, that You which hath begun a good work in me will perform it until the day of Jesus the anointed Messiah[p]:[17] Who shall separate me from the love of You the anointed Messiah[q]? shall tribulation, or distress, or persecution, or famine, or nakedness, or peril, or sword?[18]

For I am persuaded, that neither death, nor life, nor angels, nor principalities, nor powers, nor things present, nor things to come,[19] Nor height, nor depth, nor any other creature, shall be able to separate me from the love of You Theos the Godhead Trinity[r], which is in the anointed Messiah[s] Jesus my Kurios the Master[t].[20] All that the Father gives You shall come to You; and me that comes to You, You will in no wise cast out.[21] And this is the Father's will which has sent You, that of all which he has given You, You should lose nothing, but should raise it up again at the last day.[22] And this is the will of Him that sent You, that everyone which sees You the Son, and believeth on You, may have everlasting life: and You will raise him up at the last day.[23] And You give unto me eternal life; and I shall never perish, neither shall any man pluck me out of Your hand.[24] Your Father, which gave me You, is greater than all; and no man is able to pluck me out of Your Father's hand.[25]

While You were with them in the world, You kept them in Your name: those that You gave, You have kept, and none of them is lost, but the son of perdition; that the scripture might be fulfilled.[26] *I cover and seal this prayer with the Blood of Jesus. In His Name Amen.*

Scripture References

1. 1John 5:11 KJV
2. 1John 5:12 KJV.
3. 1John 5:13 KJV
4. 1John 4:13 KJV
5. Rom 8:16 KJV
6. John 1:12 KJV
7. Rom 8:14 KJV.
8. Rom 8:15 KJV
9. Rom 8:16 KJV
10. Rom 8:17 KJV
11. Eph 3:17 KJV
12. Titus 3:5 KJV
13. Eph 2:8 KJV
14. Eph 2:9 KJV
15. Rom 5:1 KJV
16. 1John 5:4 KJV
17. Phil 1:6 KJV
18. Rom 8:35 KJV
19. Rom 8:38 KJV
20. Rom 8:39 KJV
21. John 6:37 KJV
22. John 6:39 KJV
23. John 6:40 KJV
24. John 10:28 KJV
25. John 10:29 KJV
26. John 17:12 KJV

Strong's and Thayer's References

a. 1John 5:11 G2316
b. 1John 5:12 G2316
c. 1John 5:13 G2316
d. 1John 5:13 G2316
e. Rom 8:16 G2316
f. John 1:12 G2316
g. Rom 8:14 G2316
h. Rom 8:14 G2316
i. Rom 8:16 G2316
j. Rom 8:17 G2316
k. Eph 2:8 G2316
l. Rom 5:1 G2316
m. Rom 5:1 G2962
n. Rom 5:1 G5547
o. 1John 5:4 G2316
p. Phil 1:6 G5547
q. Rom 8:35 G5547
r. Rom 8:39 G2316
s. Rom 8:39 G5547
t. Rom 8:39 G2962

Being Put in The Ministry

Heavenly Father this is my prayer for being put in the ministry, according to the glorious gospel of You the blessed Theos Godhead[a], which was committed to Paul's trust,[1] and is also for me. And I thank You Christos the Anointed[b] Jehovah, Who is Salvation[c], my Kurios the Master[d], who has enabled me, and I pray that I be counted faithful, to be put into the ministry;[2] I was before a blasphemer, and a persecutor, and injurious: but I obtained mercy, because I did it ignorantly in unbelief.[3] And the grace of You our Kurios the Master[e] was exceeding abundant with faith and love which is in Christos the Anointed[f] Jehovah, Who is Salvation[g].[4]

And this is a faithful saying, and worthy of all acceptation, that You the Anointed Messiah[h], Jehovah Who is Salvation[j] came into the world to save sinners; of whom I am chief.[5] Howbeit for this cause I obtained mercy, that in me also Jehovah Who is Salvation[j], the Anointed Messiah[k] might show forth all longsuffering, for a pattern to them which should hereafter believe on You to life everlasting.[6]

Now unto You the King eternal, immortal, invisible, the only wise Theos Godhead Trinity[k], be honor and glory for ever and ever. Amen.[7] I cover and seal this prayer with the Blood of Jesus. In His Name Amen.

Scripture References

1.	1Tim 1:11 KJV	5.	1Tim 1:15 KJV
2.	1Tim 1:12 KJV	6.	1Tim 1:16 KJV
3.	1Tim 1:13 KJV	7.	1Tim 1:17 KJV
4.	1Tim 1:14 KJV		

Strong's and Thayer's References

a.	1 Tim 1:11 G2316	g.	1 Tim 1:14 G2424
b.	1 Tim 1.12 G5547	h.	1 Tim 1:15 G5447
c.	1 Tim 1:12 G2424	i.	1 Tim 1:15 G2424
d.	1 Tim 1:12 G2962	j.	1 Tim 1:16 G2424
e.	1 Tim 1:14 G2962	k.	1 Tim 1:16 G5547
f.	1 Tim 1:14 G5547	l.	1 Tim 1:17 G2316

Bless the Lord

Bless You the Self Existent Eternal Jehovah[a], O my soul, and forget not all Your benefits:[1] Blessed be You Theos the Godhead Trinity[b], even the Father of my Kurios the Master[c], Jehovah Who is Salvation[d], the Anointed Messiah[e], the Father of mercies, and You Theos the Godhead Trinity[f] of all comfort;[2] Blessed be You the Self Existent Eternal Jehovah[g] Eloheem[h], the Eloheem[i] of Israel, You who only does wondrous things.[3] Bless You the Self Existent Eternal Jehovah[j], O my soul. O Self Existent Eternal Jehovah [k]my Eloheem[l], You are very great; You are clothed with honor and majesty.[4] And blessed be Your glorious name forever: and let the whole earth be filled with Your glory; Amen, and Amen.[5]

Blessed be You the Self Existent Eternal Jehovah[m], Eloheem[n] of Israel from everlasting to everlasting: and let me and all the people say, Amen. Praise You Jah, the Lord, Most Vehement[o].[6] Blessed be You the Self Existent Eternal Jehovah[p] Eloheem[q] of Israel from everlasting, and to everlasting. Amen, and Amen.[7] Every day will I bless You; and I will praise Your name for ever and ever.[8]

Bless You the Self Existent Eternal Jehovah[r], all Your angels, that excel in strength, that do Your commandments, hearkening unto the voice of Your Word.[9] Bless You the Self Existent Eternal Jehovah[s], all Your hosts; the ministers of Your's, that do Your pleasure.[10] Bless You the Self Existent Eternal Jehovah[t], all Your works in all places of Your dominion: bless You the Self Existent Eternal Jehovah[u], O my soul.[11]

Like David I Bless You the Self Existent Eternal Jehovah[v], O my soul: and all that is within me, bless Your holy name.[12] Like David I will extol You, my Eloheem[w], O king; and I will bless Your name for ever and ever.[13] Blessed be You the Self Existent Eternal Jehovah[x] for evermore. Amen, and Amen.[14] I cover and seal this prayer with the Blood of Jesus. In His Name Amen.

Scripture References

1.	Ps 103:2 KJV	8.	Ps 145:2 KJV
2.	2Cor 1:3 KJV	9.	Ps 103:20 KJV
3.	Ps 72:18 KJV	10.	Ps 103:21 KJV
4.	Ps 104:1 KJV	11.	Ps 103:22 KJV
5.	Ps 72:19 KJV	12.	Ps 103:1 KJV
6.	Ps 106:48 KJV	13.	Ps 145:1 KJV
7.	Ps 41:13 KJV	14.	Ps 89:52 KJV

Strong's and Thayer's References

a.	Ps 103:2 H3068	m.	Ps 106:48 H3068
b.	2Cor 1:3 G2316	n.	Ps 106:48 H430
c.	2Cor 1:3 G2962	o.	Ps 106:48 H3050
d.	2Cor 1:3 G2424	p.	Ps 41:13 H3068
e.	2Cor 1:3 G5547	q.	Ps 41:13 H430
f.	2Cor 1:3 G2316	r.	Ps 103:20 H3068
g.	Ps 72:18 H3068	s.	Ps 103:21 H3068
h.	Ps 72:18 H430	t.	Ps 103:22 H3068
i.	Ps 72:18 H430	u.	Ps 103:22 H3068
j.	Ps 104:1 H3068	v.	Ps 103:1 H3068
k.	Ps 104:1 H3068	w.	Ps 145:1 H430
l.	Ps 104:1 H430	x.	Ps 89:52 H3068

Prayer for Blessing

Heavenly Father as Abraham's seed, You declare in Your Word that You call heaven and earth to record this day against me, that You have set before me life and death, blessing and cursing: therefore choose life, that both me and my seed may live:[1] And I choose life and blessing. And the scripture, foreseeing that Theos the Godhead Trinity[a] would justify the heathen through faith, preached before the gospel unto Abraham, saying, In you shall all nations be blessed.[2] Now to Abraham and his seed were the promises made. He said not, and to seeds, as of many; but as of one, and to his seed, which is Christ.[3]

And I will bless them that bless you, and curse him that curse you: and in you shall all families of the earth be blessed.[4] And all these blessings shall come on you, and overtake you, if you shall hearken unto the voice of the Self Existent Eternal Jehovah[b] your Eloheem[c].[5] And in your seed shall all the nations of the earth be blessed; because you have obeyed My voice.[6]

Blessed shall I be in the city, and blessed shall I be in the field.[7] Blessed shall be the fruit of my body, and the fruit of my ground, and the fruit of my cattle, the increase of my kine, and the flocks of my sheep.[8] Blessed shall be my basket and my store.[9] Blessed shall I be when I come in, and blessed shall I be when I go out.[10]

You the Self Existent Eternal Jehovah[d] shall command the blessing upon me in my storehouses, and in all that I set my hand to; and You shall bless me in the land which You the Self Existent Eternal Jehovah[e] my Eloheem[f] gives me.[11] I thank You Father that I am in the seed and that all these blessings are for me too.

You the Self Existent Eternal Jehovah[g] will give strength unto me one of Your people; You the Self Existent Eternal Jehovah[h] will bless me one of Your people with peace.[12] Saying, surely blessing I will bless you, and multiplying I will multiply you.[13] He that has clean hands, and a pure heart; who hath not lifted up his soul unto vanity, nor sworn deceitfully.[14] Behold, I shall be blessed because I fear You the Self Existent Eternal Jehovah[i].[15] I shall receive the blessing from You the Self Existent Eternal Jehovah[j], and righteousness from You Eloheem[k] of my salvation.[16]

And now, O Adonoy[l] Yehhovee[m], You are that Eloheem[n], and Your words be true, and You have promised this goodness unto Your servant:[17] And Jabez called on Eloheem[o] of Israel, saying, Oh that

You would bless me indeed, and enlarge my coast, and that your hand might be with me, and that thou would keep me from evil, that it may not grieve me! And You Eloheem° granted him that which he requested.[18]

And also like Jabez I pray that You would bless me indeed, and enlarge my coast, and that your hand might be with me, and that You would keep me from evil, that it may not grieve me! And please Eloheem° grant me that which I have requested. I Cover and seal this prayer with the Blood of Jesus. In His Name Amen.

Scripture References

1.	Deut 30:19 KJV	10.	Deut 28:6 KJV
2.	Gal 3:8 KJV	11.	Deut 28:8 KJV
3.	Gal 3:16 KJV	12.	Ps 29:11 KJV
4.	Gen 12:3 KJV	13.	Heb 6:14 KJV
5.	Deut 28:2 KJV	14.	Ps 24:4 KJV
6.	Gen 22:18 KJV	15.	Ps 128:4 KJV
7.	Deut 28:3 KJV	16.	Ps 24:5 KJV
8.	Deut 28:4 KJV	17.	2Sam 7:28 KJV
9.	Deut 28:5 KJV	18.	1Chr 4:10 KJV

Strong's and Thayer's References

a. Gal 3:8 G2316
b. Deut 28:2 H3068
c. Deut 28:2 H430
d. Deut 28:28 H3068
e. Deut 28:28 H3068
f. Deut 28:28 H430
g. Ps 29:11 H3068
h. Ps 29:11 H3068
i. Ps 128:4 H3068
j. Ps 24:5 H3068
k. Ps 24:5 H430
l. 2Sam 7:28 H136
m. 2Sam 7:28 H3069
n. 2Sam 7:28 H430
o. 1Chr 4:10 H430
p. 1Chr 4:10 H430

Prayer for Boldness

Abba the wicked flee when no man pursues but the righteous are bold as a lion.[1] *But You the Self Existent Eternal Jehovah*[a] *are my light and my salvation; whom shall I fear? You the Self Existent Eternal Jehovah*[b] *are the strength of my life; of whom shall I be afraid?*[2] *I shall not be afraid of evil tidings: my heart is fixed, trusting in You the Self Existent Eternal Jehovah*[c].[3]

Let my conversation be without covetousness; and let me be content with such things as I have: for You have said, You will never leave me, nor forsake me.[4] *So that I may boldly say, You Kurios the Master*[d] *are my helper, and I will not fear what man shall do to me.*[5]

And it is written when they saw the boldness of Peter and John, and perceived that they were unlearned and ignorant men, they marveled;

and they took knowledge of them, that they had been with Jesus.[6] And now, Kurios the Master[e], behold their threatening's: and grant unto your servants, that with all boldness they may speak Your Word,[7] By stretching forth their hand to heal; and that signs and wonders may be done by the name of Your holy child Jesus.[8] And Father please grant the same boldness to me to speak Your Word and that when I stretch forth my hand to heal that signs and wonders may be done through me in the Name of Jesus.

And when they had prayed, the place was shaken where they were assembled together; and they were all filled with the Holy Ghost, and they spoke the Word of You Theos the Godhead Trinity[f] with boldness.[9] And I ask that when I pray You shake things up and fill me with Holy Spirit to speak Your Word boldly.

24

And when Saul had come to Jerusalem, he tried to join himself to the disciples; but they were all afraid of him, not believing that he was a disciple.[10] *But Barnabas took him, and brought him to the apostles, and declared unto them how he had seen the Lord in the way, and that he had spoken to him, and how he had preached boldly at Damascus in the name of Jesus.*[11] *And he went into the synagogue, and spoke boldly for the space of three months, disputing and persuading the things concerning the kingdom of God.*[12]

And Father like Paul who was Saul also grant me to preach the truth of Your Kingdom with boldness. I cover and seal this prayer with the Blood of Jesus. In His Name Amen.

Scripture References

1.	Prov 28:1 KJV	7.	Acts 4:29 KJV
2.	Ps 27:1 KJV	8.	Acts 4:30 KJV
3.	Ps 112:7 KJV	9.	Acts 4:31 KJV
4.	Heb 13:5 KJV	10.	Acts 9:26 WEB
5.	Heb 13:6 KJV	11.	Acts 9:27 KJV
6.	Acts 4:13 KJV	12.	Acts 19:8 KJV

Strong's and Thayer's References

a. Ps 27:1 H3068
b. Ps 27:1 H3068
c. Ps 112:7 H3068

d. Heb 13:6 G2962
e. Acts 4:29 G2962
f. Acts 4:31 G2316

Prayer for Brotherly Love

Abba, Jesus said, He gave a new commandment to us, that we love one another; as He has loved us, that we also love one another.[1] So let us fulfill joy, and be likeminded, having the same love, being of one accord, of one mind.[2] Let nothing be done through strife or vainglory; but in lowliness of mind let each of us esteem the other better than themselves.[3] Let us look not on our own things, but let us all look on the things of others.[4] Let this mind be in us, which was also in You the Anointed Messiah[a] Jesus:[5]

Now I beseech us brethren, by the name of our Kurios the Master[b], Jesus the Anointed Messiah[c], that we all speak the same thing, and that there be no divisions among us; but that we be perfectly joined together in the same mind and in the same judgment.[6] Endeavouring to keep the unity of the Spirit in the bond of peace.[7] There is one body, and one Spirit, even as ye are called in one hope of your calling;[8]

One Kurios the Master[d], one faith, one baptism,[9] One Theos the Godhead Trinity[e] and Father of all, who is above all, and through all, and in us all.[10] Finally, brethren, farewell. Be perfect, be of good comfort, be of one mind, live in peace; and Theos the Godhead Trinity[f] of love and peace shall be with us.[11]

By this shall all men know that we are Your disciples, if we have love one to another.[12] Let brotherly love continue[13] I cover this prayer with the Blood of Jesus. In His Name Amen.

Scripture References

1. John 13:34 KJV
2. Phil 2:2 KJV
3. Phil 2:3 KJV
4. Phil 2:4 KJV
5. Phil 2:5 KJV
6. 1Cor 1:10 KJV
7. Eph 4:3 KJV
8. Eph 4:4 KJV
9. Eph 4:5 KJV
10. Eph 4:6 KJV
11. 2Cor 13:11 KJV
12. John 13:35 KJV

13.   Heb 13:1 KJV

Strong's and Thayer's References

a.   Phil 2:5 G5547
b.   1Cor 1:10 G2962
c.   1Cor 1:10 G5547

d.   Eph 4:5 G2962
e.   Eph 4:6 G2316
f.   2Cor 13:11 G2316

Prayer for Children

Abba it is written, You the Self Existent Eternal Jehovah[a] my Eloheem the Supreme God;[b] will circumcise my heart, and the heart of my offspring, to love You the Self Existent Eternal Jehovah[c] our Eloheem the Supreme God[d]; with all our heart, and with all our soul, that we may live.[1] And if it seem evil unto us to serve You the Self Existent Eternal Jehovah[e], let us choose this day who we will serve; whether the gods which our fathers served that were on the other side of the flood, or the gods of the people, in whose land you dwell: but as for me and my house, we will serve You the Self Existent Eternal Jehovah[f].[2]

And I looked, and rose up, and said unto the nobles, and to the rulers, and to the rest of the people, I will not be not afraid of them, I will remember You Eloheem the Supreme

God[g]; which is great and terrible, and I will fight for my brethren, my sons, and my daughters, my spouse, and our houses.[3] But You the Self Existent Eternal Jehovah[h], says even the captives of the mighty shall be taken away, and the prey of the terrible shall be delivered: for You will contend with them that contends with me, and You will save my children.[4]

And they shall be Your people, and You will be their Eloheem the Supreme God[i];[5] And You will give them one heart, and one way, that they may fear You forever for the good of them, and of their children after them.[6] And You will make an everlasting covenant with them, that You will not turn away from them, to do them good; but You will put Your fear in their hearts, so that they shall not depart from You[7] Yes, You will rejoice over them to do them good, and You will plant them *in this land assuredly with Your whole heart and with Your whole soul.*[8]

Please hide Your face from our sins, and blot out all our iniquities.[9] *And create in us a clean heart, O Eloheem the Supreme God;*[j] *and renew a right spirit within us.*[10] *Cast us not away from Your presence; and take not Your Holy Spirit from us*[11]. *Restore to us the joy of Your salvation; and uphold us with Your free spirit.*[12] *Then we will teach transgressors Your ways; and sinners shall be converted to You.*[13] *For we were as sheep going astray; but are now returned unto the Shepherd and Bishop of our souls.*[14] *And I have no greater joy than to hear that my children walk in truth.*[15] *I cover and seal this prayer with the Blood of Jesus. In His Name Amen.*

Scripture References

| 1. | Deut 30:6 KJV | 3. | Neh 4:14 KJV |
| 2. | Josh 24:15 KJV | 4. | Isa 49:25 KJV |

5.	Jer 32:38 KJV	11.	Ps 51:11 KJV
6.	Jer 32:39 KJV	12.	Ps 51:12 KJV
7.	Jer 32:40 KJV	13.	Ps 51:13 KJV
8.	Jer 32:41 KJV	14.	1Pet 2:25 KJV
9.	Ps 51:9 KJV	15.	3John 1:4 KJV
10.	Ps 51:10 KJV		

Strong's and Thayer's References

a.	Deut 30:6 H3068	f.	Josh 24:15 H3068
b.	Deut 30:6 H430	g.	Neh 4:14 H430
c.	Deut 30:6 H3068	h.	Isa 49:25 H3068
d.	Deut 30:6 H430	i.	Jer 32:38 H430
e.	Josh 24:15 H3068	j.	Ps 51:10 H430

Prayer for Comfort

Heavenly Father please let Your loving kindness be for my comfort, according to Your Word to your servant.[1] Yea, though I walk through the valley of the shadow of death, I will fear no evil: for You are with me; Your rod and Your staff they comfort me.[2]

You, even You, are my comforter: let me not be so poor in heart as to be in fear of man who will come to an end, and of the son of man who will be like grass?[3] Show me a sign of your goodness, that those who hate me may see it, and be shamed, because You, the Self Existent Eternal Jehovah[a], have helped me, and comforted me.[4]

Blessed be You Theos the Godhead Trinity[b], even the Father of my Kurios the Master[c], Jesus the Anointed Messiah[d], the Father of mercies, and You Theos the Godhead

Trinity[e] of all comfort;[5] You who comforts me in all my tribulation, that I may be able to comfort them which are in any trouble, by the comfort I myself am comforted with by You Theos the Godhead Trinity.[f][6] And Jesus prayed that You the Father, give me another Comforter, that He may abide with me forever;[7] But the Comforter, which is the Holy Ghost, whom the Father will send in Jesus name, He shall teach me all things, and bring all things to my remembrance, whatsoever Jesus has said unto us.[8] I cover and seal this prayer with the Blood of Jesus. In His Name Amen.

Scripture References

1.	Ps 119:76 WEB	5.	2Cor 1:3 KJV
2.	Ps 23:4 KJV	6.	2Cor 1:4 KJV
3.	Isa 51:12 BBE	7.	John 14:16 KJV
4.	Ps 86:17 WEB	8.	John 14:26 KJV

Strong's and Thayer's References

a.	Ps 86:17 H3068	d.	2Cor 1:3 G5547
b.	2Cor 1:3 G3216	e.	2Cor 1:3 G3216
c.	2 Cor 1:3 G2962	f.	2Cor 1:4 G3216

35

Prayer for Contentment

Heavenly Father I cast my burden upon You the Self Existent Eternal Jehovah[a], and You shall sustain me: You shall never suffer the righteous to be moved.[1] I am casting all my care upon You; for You care for me.[2] A sound heart is the life of the flesh: but envy the rottenness of the bones.[3] So let not envy rise up in me. Let my conversation be without covetousness; and let me be content with such things as I have: for You have said, You will never leave me, or forsake me.[4] So that I may boldly say, You Kurios the Master[b] are my helper, and I will not fear what man shall do unto me.[5]

Not that I speak in respect of want: for I have learned, in whatsoever state I am in to be content.[6] Let me know both how to be abased, and how to abound: everywhere and in all things I am instructed both to be *full and to be hungry, both to abound and to suffer need.*[7] *And a merry heart does good like medicine: but a broken spirit dries the bones.*[8] *So let me have a merry heart. And godliness with contentment is great gain.*[9] *For I brought nothing into this world, and it is certain I can carry nothing out.*[10] *So with having food and raiment let me be content.*[11] *I cover and seal this prayer with the Blood of Jesus. In His Name Amen.*

Scripture References

1.	Ps 55:22 KJV	7.	Phil 4:12 KJV
2.	1Pet 5:7 KJV	8.	Prov 17:22 KJV
3.	Prov 14:30 KJV	9.	1Tim 6:6 KJV
4.	Heb 13:5 KJV	10.	1Tim 6:7 KJV
5.	Heb 13:6 KJV	11.	1Tim 6:8 KJV
6.	Phil 4:11 KJV		

Strong's and Thayer's References

a.	Ps 55:22 H3068	b.	Heb 13:6 G2962

Prayer for Courage

Heavenly Father, it is written no matter what the land is that I dwell in, whether it be good or bad; and what cities that I dwell in, whether in tents, or in strong holds;[1] You have commanded me to be strong and of a good courage; be not afraid, neither be dismayed: for You the Self Existent Eternal Jehovah,[a] my Eloheem[b] are with me wherever I go.[2] For You the Self Existent Eternal Jehovah[c], my Eloheem[d] go with me, to fight for me against my enemies, to save me.[3]

When I am in tribulation, and all these things (captivity, thraldom[t], hard labour, and want of the necessaries of life)[u] have come upon me even in the latter days, if I turn to You the Self Existent Eternal Jehovah[e], my Eloheem[f], and shall be obedient unto Your voice;[4] (For You the Self Existent Eternal Jehovah

[g]my *Eloheem*[h] are the merciful *Almighty*[i];) You will not forsake me, neither destroy me, nor forget the covenant of my fathers which You swore unto them.[5]

So let me be of good courage, and let me behave myself valiantly for my people, and for the cities of my *Eloheem*[j]: and let You the Self Existent Eternal Jehovah [k]do that which is good in Your sight.[6]

I will not fear for You are with me or be not dismayed; for You are my *Eloheem*[l]: You will strengthen me; yes, You will help me; yes, You will uphold me with the right hand of Your righteousness.[7] So that I may boldly say, You *Kurios* the *Master*[m] are my helper, and I will not fear what man shall do unto me.[8]

I wait on You the Self Existent Eternal *Jehovah*[n]: be of good courage, and You shall strengthen my heart: wait, I say, on You the Self Existent

Eternal Jehovah[o].[9] Be of good courage, and You shall strengthen my heart, I hope in You the Self Existent Eternal Jehovah[p].[10] You the Self Existent Eternal Jehovah[q] of hosts is with me; You the Eloheem[r] of Jacob are my refuge. Selah.[11]

Finally, I will, be strong in You Kurios the Master[s], and in the power of Your might.[12] I cover and seal this prayer with the Blood of Jesus. In His Name Amen.

Scripture References

1.	Num 13:19 KJV	7.	Isa 41:10 KJV
2.	Josh 1:9 KJV	8.	Heb 13:6 KJV
3.	Deut 20:4 KJV	9.	Ps 27:14 KJV
4.	Deut 4:30 KJV	10.	Ps 31:24 KJV
5.	Deut 4:31 [KJV	11.	Ps 46:11 KJV
6.	1Chr 19:13 [KJV	12.	Eph 6:10 KJV

Strong's, Thayer's, John Gill's, Webster's References

a.	Josh 1:9 H3068	j.	1Chr 19:13 H430
b.	Josh 1:9 H430	k.	1Chr 19:13 H3068
c.	Deut 20:4 H3068	l.	Isa 41:10 H430
d.	Duet 20:4 H430	m.	Heb 13:6 H2962
e.	Deut 4:30 H3068	n.	Ps 27:14 H3068
f.	Duet 4:30 H430	o.	Ps 27:14 H3068
g.	Deut 4:31 H3068	p.	Ps 31:24 H3068
h.	Duet 4:31 H430	q.	Ps 46:11 H3068
i.	Duet 4:31 H410	r.	Ps 46:11 H430

s. Eph 6:10 H2962

t. Webster's: slavery; bondage; a state of servitude

u. John.Gill's: captivity, thraldom, hard labour, and want of the necessaries of life

Deliverance from Enemies

Father You the Self Existent Eternal Jehovah[a] my Eloheem[b] are the one that goes with me, to fight for me against my enemies, to save me.[1] You are the Eloheem[c] of my rock; in You will I trust: You are my shield, and the horn of my salvation, my high tower, and my refuge, my Saviour; You save me from violence.[2] I will call on You the Self Existent Eternal Jehovah[d], who is worthy to be praised: so shall I be saved from mine enemies.[3]

And You the Self Existent Eternal Jehovah[e] shall help me, and deliver me: You shall deliver me from the wicked, and save me, because I trust in You.[4] You deliver me from my enemies: yes, You lift me up above those that rise up against me: You have delivered me from the violent man.[5] When the wicked, even my enemies and my foes, came upon me to eat up my flesh, they stumbled and fell.[6] Though a host should encamp against me, my heart shall not fear: though war should rise against me, in this will I be confident.[7] One thing have I desired of you the Self Existent Eternal Jehovah[f], that will I seek after; that I may dwell in the house of you the Self Existent Eternal Jehovah[g] all the days of my life, to behold the beauty of you the Self Existent Eternal Jehovah[h], and to enquire in your temple.[8] For in the time of trouble you shall hide me in your pavilion: in the secret of your tabernacle shall you hide me; you shall set me up upon a rock.[9]

And now shall my head be lifted up above my enemies round about me: therefore will I offer in your tabernacle sacrifices of joy; I will sing, yes, I will sing praises unto you the Self Existent Eternal Jehovah[i].[10] Hear, O Self Existent Eternal

43

Jehovah[j], when I cry with my voice: have mercy also upon me, and answer me.[11]

You the Self Existent Eternal Jehovah[k] shall cause my enemies that rise up against me to be smitten before my face: they shall come out against me one way, and flee before me seven ways.[12] But You the Self Existent Eternal Jehovah[l], my Eloheem[m] I shall fear; and You shall deliver me out of the hand of all my enemies.[13] Deliver me, O Self Existent Eternal Jehovah[n], from my enemies: I flee unto You to hide me.[14] O my Eloheem[o], I trust in You: let me not be ashamed, let not my enemies triumph over me.[15] By this I know that You favor me, because my enemy does not triumph over me.[16] I trust in You, O Self Existent Eternal Jehovah[p]: I said, You are my Eloheem[q].[17] My times are in Your hand: deliver me from the hand of my enemies, and from them that persecute me.[18]

Make Your face to shine upon me Your servant: save me for Your mercies' sake.[19] Let not them that are my enemies wrongfully rejoice over me: neither let them wink with the eye that hate me without a cause.[20] My enemies would daily swallow me up: for they be many that fight against me, O You most High.[21] What time I am afraid, I will trust in You.[22]

In You Eloheem[r] I will praise Your Word, in You Eloheem[s] I have put my trust; I will not fear what flesh can do unto me.[23] When I cry unto You, then shall my enemies turn back: this I know; for You Eloheem[t] are for me.[24] In You Eloheem[u] will I praise Your Word: in You the Self Existent Eternal Jehovah[v] will I praise Your Word.[25] You through Your commandments have made me wiser than my enemies: for they are ever with me.[26]

I have more understanding than all my teachers: for Your testimonies are my meditation.[27] I understand more than the ancients, because I keep Your precepts.[28] You the Self Existent Eternal Jehovah[w] are my rock, and my fortress, and my deliverer; my El the Almighty[x], my strength, in whom I will trust; my buckler, and the horn of my salvation, and my high tower.[29]

I will call upon You the Self Existent Eternal Jehovah[y], who is worthy to be praised: so shall I be saved from my enemies.[30] It is You El the Almighty[z] that avenges me, and that brings down the people under me,[31] And that brings me forth from my enemies: You also have lifted me up on high above them that rose up against me: You have delivered me from the violent man.[32] Therefore I will give thanks unto You, O Self Existent Eternal Jehovah[aa], among the heathen, and I will sing praises unto Your name.[33]

You prepare a table before me in the presence of my enemies: You anoint my head with oil; my cup runs over.[34] Surely goodness and mercy shall follow me all the days of my life: and I will dwell in Your house, the Self Existent Eternal Jehovah[bb] forever.[35] I cover and seal this prayer with the Blood of Jesus. In His Name Amen.

Scripture References

1.	Deut 20:4 KJV	18.	Ps 31:15 KJV
2.	2Sam 22:3 KJV	19.	Ps 31:16 KJV
3.	2Sam 22:4 KJV	20.	Ps 35:19 KJV
4.	Ps 37:40 KJV	21.	Ps 56:2 KJV
5.	Ps 18:48 KJV	22.	Ps 56:3 KJV
6.	Ps 27:2 KJV	23.	Ps 56:4 KJV
7.	Ps 27:3 KJV	24.	Ps 56:9 KJV
8.	Ps 27:4 KJV	25.	Ps 56:10 KJV
9.	Ps 27:5 KJV	26.	Ps 119:98 KJV
10.	Ps 27:6 KJV	27.	Ps 119:99 KJV
11.	Ps 27:7 KJV	28.	Ps 119:100 KJV
12.	Deut 28:7 KJV	29.	Ps 18:2 KJV
13.	2Kgs 17:39 KJV	30.	Ps 18:3 KJV
14.	Ps 143:9 KJV	31.	2Sam 22:48 KJV
15.	Ps 25:2 KJV	32.	2Sam 22:49 KJV
16.	Ps 41:11 KJV	33.	2Sam 22:50 KJV
17.	Ps 31:14 KJV	34.	Ps 23:5 KJV

35.   Ps 23:6 KJV

Strong's and Thayer's References

a.   Deut 20:4 H3068
b.   Duet 20:4 H430
c.   2Sam 22:3 H430
d.   2Sam 22:4 H3068
e.   Ps 37:40 H3068
f.   Ps 27:4 H3068
g.   Ps 27:4 H3068
h.   Ps 27:4 H3068
i.   Ps 27:6 H3068
j.   Ps 27:7 H3068
k.   Deut 28:7 H3068
l.   2Kgs 17:39 H3068
m.   2Kgs 17:39 H430
n.   Ps 143:9 H3068

o.   Ps 25:2 H430
p.   Ps 31:14 H3068
q.   Ps 31:14 H430
r.   Ps 56:4 H430
s.   Ps 56:4 H430
t.   Ps 56:9 H430
u.   Ps 56:10 H430
v.   Ps 56:10 H3068
w.   Ps 18:2 H3068
x.   Ps 18:2 H410
y.   Ps 18:3 H3068
z.   2Sam 22:48 H410
aa.   2Sam 22:50 H3068
bb.   Ps 23:6 H3068

48

Prayer for Deliverance

Heavenly Father I am troubled on every side, yet not distressed; I am perplexed, but not in despair;[1] *Persecuted, but not forsaken; cast down, but not destroyed;*[2] *Many are the afflictions of the righteous: but You the Self Existent Eternal Jehovah*[a] *deliver me out of them all.*[3] *As my fathers trusted in You: I trust in You, and You do deliver me.*[4] *I cry unto You, and am delivered: I trust in You, and am not confounded.*[5]

In my distress I call upon You the Self Existent Eternal Jehovah[b]*, and cry unto You my Eloheem*[c]*: You hear my voice out of Your temple, and my cry comes before You, even into Your ears.*[6]

You deliver me from my strong enemy, and from them which hate me: for they are too strong for me.[7] *You the Self Existent Eternal Jehovah*[d] *are my rock, and my*

49

fortress, and my deliverer; my El the Almighty[e], my strength, in whom I will trust; my buckler, and the horn of my salvation, and my high tower.[8] I wait patiently for You the Self Existent Eternal Jehovah[f]; and You incline unto me, and hear my cry.[9] You bring me up also out of an horrible pit, out of the miry clay, and set my feet upon a rock, and establish my goings.[10] And You put a new song in my mouth, even praise unto You my Eloheem[g]: many shall see it, and fear, and shall trust in You the Self Existent Eternal Jehovah[h].[11]

Because I have set my love upon You, therefore You will deliver me: You will set me on high, because I have known Your name.[12] I shall call upon You, and You will answer me: You will be with me in trouble; You will deliver me, and honor me.[13] With long life will You satisfy me, and show me Your salvation.[14] I sought You the Self Existent Eternal Jehovah[i], and You hear me, and deliver me from all my fears.[15] You sent Your Word, and healed me, and delivered me from destructions.[16] I cover and seal this prayer with the Blood of Jesus. In His Name Amen.

Scripture References

1.	2Cor 4:8 KJV	9.	Ps 40:1 KJV
2.	2Cor 4:9 KJV	10.	Ps 40:2 KJV
3.	Ps 34:19 KJV	11.	Ps 40:3 KJV
4.	Ps 22:4 KJV	12.	Ps 91:14 KJV
5.	Ps 22:5 KJV	13.	Ps 91:15 KJV
6.	Ps 18:6 KJV	14.	Ps 91:16 KJV
7.	Ps 18:17 KJV	15.	Ps 34:4 KJV
8.	Ps 18:2 KJV	16.	Ps 107:20 KJV

Strong's and Thayer's references

a.	Ps 34:19 H3068	f.	Ps 40:1 H3068
b.	Ps 18:6 H3068	g.	Ps 40:3 H430
c.	Ps 18:6 H430	h.	Ps 40:3 H3068
d.	Ps 18:2 H3068	i.	Ps 34:4 H3068
e.	Ps 18:2 H410		

Prayer for Direction

Heavenly Father, I come in Jesus Name to seek your direction, I have a plan but I trust You Jehovah the Self Existent Eternal[a] to direct my steps.[1] So please take, O Jehovah the existing one[b], the free offerings of my mouth, and give me knowledge of Your decisions.[2] The law of Your mouth is better unto me than thousands of gold and silver.[3] Let my steps be guided by Your Word; and let not sin have control over me.[4] Lead me in Your truth, and teach me: for You are Eloheem[c] of my salvation; on You do I wait all the day.[5]

Make Your way clear to me, O Jehovah the Self Existent Eternal[d]; I will go on my way in Your faith: let my heart be glad in the fear of Your name.[6] Give me knowledge and good sense; for I have put my faith in Your teachings.[7] Make the way of

Your orders clear to me; then my thoughts will be ever on Your wonders.[8] Your Word is a lamp unto my feet, and a light unto my path.[9] But all things, when their true quality is seen, are made clear by the light: because everything which is made clear is light.[10] You, O Jehovah the Self Existent Eternal One[e], will be my light; by You, my Eloheem[f], the dark will be made bright for me.[11] Thank You that my steps are established by You Jehovah the Self Existent Eternal One[g], and he delights in his way.[12] Hold up my goings in Your paths, that my footsteps slip not.[13] And righteousness will go before me and prepare the way for my steps.[14]

I thank You that when I go, my way will not be narrow, and in running I will not have a fall.[15] I cover and seal this prayer with the Blood of Jesus. In His Name Amen.

Scripture References

1. Prov 16:9 KJV
2. Ps 119::108 BBE
3. Ps 119:72 KJV
4. Ps 119:133 BBE
5. Ps 25:5 KJV
6. Ps 86:11 BBE
7. Ps 119:66 BBE
8. Ps 119:27 BBE
9. Ps 119:105 KJV
10. Eph 5:13 BBE
11. Ps 18:28 BBE
12. Ps 37:23 BBE
13. Ps 17:5 KJV
14. Ps 85:13 WEB
15. Prov 4:12 BBE

Strong's and Thayer's References

a. Prov 16:9 H3068
b. Ps 119:108 H3068
c. Ps 25:5 H430
d. Ps 86:11 H3068
e. Ps 18:28 H3068
f. Ps 18:28 H430
g. Ps 37:23 H3068

Acceptable Fasting

Father in heaven it is written, Is it such a fast that You have chosen? a day for a man to afflict his soul? is it to bow down his head as a bulrush, and to spread sackcloth and ashes under him? will I call this a fast, and an acceptable day to You the Self Existent Eternal Jehovah[a]?[1]

Is not this the fast that You have chosen? to loose the bands of wickedness, to undo the heavy burdens, and to let the oppressed go free, and that I break every yoke?[2] Is it not to deal my bread to the hungry, and that I bring the poor that are cast out to my house? when I see the naked, that I cover him; and that I hide not myself from my own flesh?[3] Then shall my light break forth as the morning, and my health shall spring forth speedily: and my righteousness shall go before me; the glory of You the Self Existent

Eternal Jehovah[b] *shall be my reward.*[4]

Then shalt I call, and You the Self Existent Eternal Jehovah[c] *shall answer; I shall cry, and You shall say, Here I am. If I take away from the midst of me the yoke, the putting forth of the finger, and speaking vanity;*[5] *And if I draw out my soul to the hungry, and satisfy the afflicted soul; then shall my light rise in obscurity, and my darkness be as the noonday:*[6]

And You the Self Existent Eternal Jehovah[d] *shall guide me continually, and satisfy my soul in drought, and make fat my bones: and I shall be like a watered garden, and like a spring of water, whose waters fail not.*[7]

Moreover when I fast, be not, as the hypocrites, of a sad countenance: for they disfigure their faces, that they may appear unto men to fast. Verily

Jesus says unto me, They have their reward.[8] *But me, when I fast, anoint my head, and wash my face;*[9] *That I appear not unto men to fast, but unto You my Father which is in secret: and You my Father, which sees in secret, shall reward me openly.*[10] *I cover and seal this prayer with the Blood of Jesus. In His Name Amen.*

Scripture References

1.	Isa 58:5 KJV	6.	Isa 58:10 KJV
2.	Isa 58:6 KJV	7.	Isa 58:11 KJV
3.	Isa 58:7 KJV	8.	Matt 6:16 KJV
4.	Isa 58:8 KJV	9.	Matt 6:17 KJV
5.	Isa 58:9 KJV	10.	Matt 6:18 KJV

Strong's and Thayer's References

a.	Isa 58:5 H3068	c.	Isa 58:9 H3068
b.	Isa 58:8 H3068	d.	Isa 58:11 H3068

Prayer for Favor

Abba I seek Your favor with my whole heart: be merciful unto me according to Your Word.¹ For You, the Self Existent Eternal Jehovahᵃ, wilt bless the righteous; with favor and compass him as with a shield.² And a good man obtains favor from You the Self Existent Eternal Jehovahᵇ: but a man of wicked devices will he condemn.³

Let me not yield to any wicked devices. Let not mercy and truth forsake me: bind them about my neck; write them upon the table of my heart.⁴ So shall I find favor and good understanding in the sight of You Eloheemᶜ and man.⁵

Now like You Eloheemᵈ had brought Daniel into favor and tender love with the prince of the eunuchs.⁶ And You the Self Existent Eternal Jehovahᵉ were with Joseph, and showed him mercy, and gave him favor in the sight of the keeper of the prison.[7] And like the child Samuel grew on, and was in favor both with You the Self Existent Eternal Jehovah[f], and also with men.[8] And like Jesus increased in wisdom and stature, and in favor with You Theos the Godhead Trinity[g] and man.[9] I ask for You to bring me into favor with all officials and leaders that I may have dealings with or who You have placed over me and I ask to grow in favor with You and all people.

So please remember me, O Self Existent Eternal Jehovah[h], with the favor that You show to Your people: O visit me with Your salvation;[10]

And I say, my Adonoy[i], if now I have found favor in Your sight, pass not away, I pray, from me Your servant:[11] You the Self Existent Eternal Jehovah[j], by Your favor You have made my mountain to stand strong: You did hide Your face, and I *was troubled.*[12] *But You shall arise, and have mercy upon Zion: for the time to favor her, yes, the set time, is come.*[13] *I thank You for Favor.*

I cover and seal this prayer with the Blood of Jesus. In His Name Amen.

Scripture References

1.	Ps 119:58 KJV	7.	Gen 39:21 KJV
2.	Ps 5:12 KJV	8.	1Sam 2:26 KJV
3.	Prov 12:2 KJV	9.	Luke 2:52 KJV
4.	Prov 3:3 KJV	10.	Ps 106:4 KJV
5.	Prov 3:4 KJV	11.	Gen 18:3 KJV
6.	Dan 1:9 KJV	12.	Ps 30:7 KJV

Strong's and Thayer's References

a.	Ps 5:12 H3068	f.	1Sam 2:26 H3068
b.	Prov 12:2 H3068	g.	Luke 2:52 G2316
c.	Prov 3:4 H430	h.	Ps 106:4 H3068
d.	Dan 1:9 H430	i.	Gen 18:3 H136
e.	Gen 39:21 H3068	j.	Ps 30:7 H3068

Prayer for Forgiving

Father in heaven please forgive me my debts, as I forgive my debtors.[1] And when I stand praying, I forgive, if I have ought against any: that You my Father also which are in heaven may forgive me my trespasses.[2] But if I do not forgive, neither will You my Father which is in heaven forgive my trespasses.[3] Let me be kind to others, tenderhearted, forgiving them, even as You Theos the Godhead Trinity[a] for Christ's sake has forgiven me.[4]

Let me be forbearing with others, and forgiving others, if I have a quarrel against any: even as the Anointed Messiah[b] forgave me, so also do I.[5] For if I forgive men their trespasses, You my heavenly Father will also forgive me.[6] But if I forgive not men their trespasses, neither will You my Father forgive my trespasses.[7] For if I have no mercy I will be judged without mercy, but mercy takes pride in overcoming judging.[8] *But Jesus says unto me, to love my enemies, bless them that curse me, do good to them that hate me, and pray for them which despitefully use me, and persecute me;*[9] *That I may be a child of You my Father which is in heaven: for You make Your sun to rise on the evil and on the good, and sends rain on the just and on the unjust.*[10]

If I am angry I will sin not: let not the sun go down upon my wrath:[11] *Neither give place to the devil.*[12] *But I love my enemies, and do good, and lend, hoping for nothing again; and my reward shall be great, and I shall be a child of Your's the Highest: for You are kind unto the unthankful and to the evil.*[13] *I will be therefore merciful, as You my Father is also merciful.*[14] *Let me judge not, and I shall not be judged: condemn not, and I shall not be condemned: forgive, and I shall be forgiven:*[15]

Give, and it shall be given unto me; good measure, pressed down, and shaken together, and running over, shall men give into my bosom. For with the same measure that I mete with all it shall be measured to me again.[16] *I cover and seal this prayer with the Blood of Jesus. In His Name Amen.*

Scripture References

1.	Matt 6:12 KJV	9.	Matt 5:44 KJV
2.	Mark 11:25 KJV	10.	Matt 5:45 KJV
3.	Mark 11:26 KJV	11.	Eph 4:26 KJV
4.	Eph 4:32 KJV	12.	Eph 4:27 KJV
5.	Col 3:13 KJV	13.	Luke 6:35 KJV
6.	Matt 6:14 KJV	14.	Luke 6:36 KJV
7.	Matt 6:15 KJV	15.	Luke 6:37 KJV
8.	Jas 2:13 BBE	16.	Luke 6:38 KJV

Strong's and Thayer's References

a.	Eph 4:32 G2316	b.	Col 3:13 G5547

Prayer for Friends

Abba it is written a man that has friends must show himself friendly: and there is a friend that sticks closer than a brother.[1] And to make no friendship with an angry man; and with a furious man you shall not go:[2] Lest you learn his ways, and get a snare to your soul.[3] So I show myself friendly but will not make friends with angry people so I do not become like them. As a friend is loving at all times, and becomes a brother in times of trouble.[4] So I choose to be a loving friend and be there like a brother when my friend has troubles.

And let me be moving one another at all times to love and good works;[5] Not giving up my meetings, as is the way of some, but keeping one another strong in faith; and all the more because I see the day coming near.[6] And faithful are the wounds of a friend; but the kisses of an enemy are deceitful.[7]

So let me always speak the truth in Love. Although oil and perfume make glad the heart, let me listen to the wise suggestion of a friend because it is sweet to my soul.[8]

Now I make request to you, my brothers, in the name of our Kurios the Master[a], Jesus the Anointed, Messiah[b], that my friends and I say the same thing, and that there may be no divisions among us, so that we may be in complete agreement, in the same mind and in the same opinion [9] with the truth.

So that even when my dearest friend, in whom I had faith, who took bread with me, is turned against me.[10] Let me be gentle to others and have forgiveness for others, if anyone has done wrong to his brother, even as you the anointed Messiah[c] has forgiveness *for us:*[11] *And more than all, have love; the only way in which we may be completely joined together.*[12]

And let the peace of Christ be ruling in our hearts, as it was the purpose of You Theos the Godhead Trinity[c] *for us to be one body; and give praise to You God at all times.*[13] *I cover and seal this prayer with the Blood of Jesus. In His Name Amen.*

Scripture References

1. Prov 18:24 KJV
2. Prov 22:24 KJV
3. Prov 22:25 KJV
4. Prov 17:17 BBE
5. Heb 10:24 BBE
6. Heb 10:25 BBE
7. Prov 27:6 KJV
8. Prov 27:9 BBE
9. 1Co 1:10 BBE
10. Ps 41:9 BBE
11. Col 3:13 BBE
12. Col 3:14 BBE
13. Col 3:15 BBE

Strong's and Thayer's References

a. 1Cor 1:10 G2962
b. 1Cor 1:10 G5547
c. Col 3:13 G5547
d. Col 3:15 G2316

Prayer for Guidance

Heavenly Father cause me to hear Your loving kindness in the morning; for in You do I trust: cause me to know the way wherein I should walk; for I lift up my soul unto You.[1] You restore my soul: You lead me in the paths of righteousness for Your name's sake.[2]

Teach me to do Your will; for You are my Eloheem[a]: Your spirit is good; lead me into the land of uprightness.[3] You will guide the humble in justice. You will teach the humble his way.[4]

All the paths of You the Self Existent Eternal Jehovah[b] are mercy and truth unto such as keep Your covenant and Your testimonies.[5] Make me to go in the path of Your commandments; for therein do I delight.[6]

Thus says You the Self Existent Eternal Jehovah[c], my Redeemer, the

Holy One of Israel; I am the Self Existent Eternal Jehovah[d] Your Eloheem[e] which teaches you to profit, which leads you by the way that you should go.[7] You will instruct me and teach me in the way which I shall go: You will guide me with Your eye.[8] You lead in the way of righteousness, in the midst of the paths of judgment:[9]

I shall observe to do therefore as You the Self Existent Eternal Jehovah[f] my Eloheem[g] has commanded me: I shall not turn aside to the right hand or to the left.[10] And my ears shall hear a word behind me, saying, This is the way, walk in it, when I turn to the right hand, and when I turn to the left.[11]

I trust in You the Self Existent Eternal Jehovah[h] with all my heart; and lean not unto my own understanding.[12] In all my ways I acknowledge You, and You shall direct thy paths.[13]

And You the Self Existent Eternal Jehovah[i] shall guide me continually, and satisfy my soul in drought, and make fat my bones: and I shalt be like a watered garden, and like a spring of water, whose waters fail not.[14]

The steps of a good man are ordered by You the Self Existent Eternal Jehovah[j]: and he delights in his way.[15] *And I know that all things work together for good to me because I love You Theos the Godhead Trinity[k], to me who is called according to Your purpose.*[16] *I cover and seal this prayer with the Blood of Jesus. In His Name Amen.*

Scripture References

1.	Ps 143:8 KJV	7.	Isa 48:17 KJV
2.	Ps 23:3 KJV	8.	Ps 32:8 KJV
3.	Ps 143:10 KJV	9.	Prov 8:20 KJV
4.	Ps 25:9 WEB	10.	Deut 5:32 KJV
5.	Ps 25:10 KJV	11.	Isa 30:21 KJV
6.	Ps 119:35 KJV	12.	Prov 3:5 KJV

69

| 13. | Prov 3:6 KJV | 15. | Ps 37:23 KJV |
| 14. | Isa 58:11 KJV | 16. | Rom 8:28 KJV |

Strong's and Thayer's References

a.	Ps 143:10 H430	g.	Duet 5:32 H430
b.	Ps 25:10 H3068	h.	Prov 3:5 H3068
c.	Isa 48:17 H3068	i.	Isa 58:11 H3068
d.	Isa 48:17 H3068	j.	Ps 37:23 H3068
e.	Isa 48:17 H430	k.	Rom 8:28 G2316
f.	Deut 5:32 H3068		

Have No Fear

Heavenly Father it is written that You Theos the Godhead Trinity[z] have not given me the spirit of fear; but of power, and of love, and of a sound mind.[1] For I have not received the spirit of bondage again to fear; but I have received the Spirit of adoption, whereby I cry, Abba, Father.[2] For You the Self Existent Eternal Jehovah[b] my Eloheem[c] will hold my right hand, saying unto me, Fear not; You will help me.[3] I will not fear; for You are with me: I will be not dismayed; for You are my Eloheem[d]: You will strengthen me; yes, You will help me; yes, You will uphold me with the right hand of Your righteousness.[4]

Behold, You El the Almighty[e] are my salvation; I will trust, and not be afraid: for You Yaw the Lord most Vehement[f] the Self Existent Eternal Jehovah[g] are my strength and my

71

song; You also have become my salvation.[5] Have You not commanded me? Be strong and of a good courage; be not afraid, neither be dismayed: for You the Self Existent Eternal Jehovah[h] my Eloheem[i] are with me where ever I go.[6] The fear of man brings a snare: but I put my trust in You the Self Existent Eternal Jehovah[j] and shall be safe.[7] You the Self Existent Eternal Jehovah[k] are on my side; I will not fear: what can man do unto me?[8]

You have a mighty arm: strong is Your hand, and high is Your right hand.[9] Justice and judgment are the habitation of Your throne: mercy and truth shall go before Your face.[10] In righteousness shall I be established: I shall be far from oppression; for I shall not fear: and from terror; for it shall not come near me.[11] You the Self Existent Eternal Jehovah[l] are my light and my salvation; whom shall I fear? You the Self Existent Eternal Jehovah[m] are the strength of my life; of whom shall I be afraid?[12]

If I listen to You I will dwell securely, and will be at ease, without fear of harm.[13] I shall not be afraid of evil tidings: my heart is fixed, trusting in You the Self Existent Eternal Jehovah[n].[14] What time I am afraid, I will trust in You.[15] You will keep me in perfect peace, because my mind is stayed on You: because I trust in You.[16] I sought You the Self Existent Eternal Jehovah[o], and You heard me, and delivered me from all my fears.[17] I cover and seal this prayer with the Blood of Jesus. In His Name Amen.

Scripture References

1.	2Tim 1:7 KJV	9.	Ps 89:13 KJV
2.	Rom 8:15 KJV	10.	Ps 89:14 KJV
3.	Isa 41:13 KJV	11.	Isa 54:14 KJV
4.	Isa 41:10 KJV	12.	Ps 27:1 KJV
5.	Isa 12:2 KJV	13.	Prov 1:33 WEB
6.	Josh 1:9 KJV	14.	Ps 112:7 KJV
7.	Prov 29:25 KJV	15.	Ps 56:3 KJV
8.	Ps 118:6 KJV	16.	Isa 26:3 KJV

17.   Ps 34:4 KJV

Strong's and Thayer's References

a.   2Tim 1:7 G2316
b.   Isa 41:13 H3068
c.   Isa 41:13 H430
d.   Isa 41:10 H430
e.   Isa 12:2 H410
f.   Isa 12:2 H3050
g.   Isa 12:2 H3068
h.   Josh 1:9 H3068
i.   Josh 1:9 H430
j.   Prov 29:25 H3068
k.   Ps 118:6 H3068
l.   Ps 27:1 H3068
m.   Ps 27:1 H3068
n.   Ps 112:7 H3068
o.   Ps 34:4 H3068

Prayer for Healing

Jehovah[a] Rapha[b], I come in Jesus Name and ask that You heal me, Jehovah, the Self Existent Eternal One[c], and I shall be healed; save me, and I shall be saved: for You are my praise.[1] It is written, You Jesus were wounded for my transgressions, You were bruised for my iniquities: the chastisement of my peace was upon You; and with Your stripes I am healed.[2] You took my sins on Yourself, giving Your body to be nailed on the tree, so that I, being dead to sin, might have a new life in righteousness, and by Your wounds I have been made well.[3]

Let me, give attention to Your words; let my ear be turned to Your sayings.[4] Let them not go from my eyes; keep them deep in my heart.[5] For they are life to me, and strength to all my flesh.[6] Let me speak pleasant words as a honeycomb, sweet to my soul, and health to my bones.[7] Make my mouth full of good things, so that my strength is made new again like the eagle's.[8] You Jehovah, the Self Existent Eternal One[d], my Eloheem[e]! I cry out to you and you heal me.[9] I cover and seal this prayer with the Blood of Jesus. In His Name Amen.

Scripture References

1.	Jer 17:14 KJV		6.	Prov 4:22 BBE
2.	Isa 53:5 KJV		7.	Prov 16:24 KJV
3.	1 Pet 2:24 BBE		8.	Ps 103:5 BBE
4.	Prov 4:20 BBE		9.	Ps 30:2 KJV
5.	Prov 4:21 BBE			

Strong's and Thayer's References

a.	H3068		d.	Ps 30:2 H3068
b.	H7495		e.	Ps 30:2 H430
c.	Jer 17:14 3068			

Help in Troubles

O Self Existent Eternal Jehovah[a], be gracious unto me; I have waited for You: be my arm every morning, my salvation also in the time of trouble.[1] Hide not Your face from me in the day when I am in trouble; incline Your ear unto me: in the day when I call, answer me speedily.[2]

You the Self Existent Eternal Jehovah[b] will also be a refuge if I am oppressed, a refuge in times of trouble.[3] I shall call upon You, and You will answer me: You will be with me in trouble; You will deliver me, and honor me[4] You are my hiding place; You shall preserve me from trouble; You shalt compass me about with songs of deliverance. Selah.[5]

Deliver me, O Self Existent Eternal Jehovah[c], from my enemies: I flee unto You to hide me.[6] For in the time of trouble You shall hide me in Your *pavilion: in the secret of Your tabernacle shall You hide me; You shall set me up upon a rock.⁷ You shall deliver me in six troubles: yes, in seven there shall no evil touch me.⁸ But the salvation of the righteous is of You the Self Existent Eternal Jehovah*ᵈ*: You are my strength in the time of trouble.⁹ And You the Self Existent Eternal Jehovah*ᵉ *shall help me, and deliver me: You shall deliver me from the wicked, and save me, because I trust in You.¹⁰*

*Though I fall, I shall not be utterly cast down: for You the Self Existent Eternal Jehovah*ᵍ *uphold me with Your hand.¹¹ And I that know Your name will put my trust in You: for You, the Self Existent Eternal Jehovah*ʰ*, have not forsaken me because I seek You.¹² And call upon You in the day of trouble: You will deliver me, and I shall glorify You.¹³*

You the Self Existent Eternal Jehovah[i] is nigh unto me that calls upon You, I call upon You in truth.[14] You are my hiding place and my shield: I hope in Your Word.[15] I cover and seal this prayer with the Blood of Jesus. In His Name Amen.

Scripture References

1.	Isa 33:2 KJV	9.	Ps 37:39 KJV
2.	Ps 102:2 KJV	10.	Ps 37:40 KJV
3.	Ps 9:9 KJV	11.	Ps 37:24 KJV
4.	Ps 91:15 KJV	12.	Ps 9:10 KJV
5.	Ps 32:7 KJV	13.	Ps 50:15 KJV
6.	Ps 143:9 KJV	14.	Ps 145:18 KJV
7.	Ps 27:5 KJV	15.	Ps 119:114 KJV
8.	Job 5:19 KJV		

Strong's and Thayer's References

a.	Isa 33:2 H3068	f.	Ps 37:23 H3068
b.	Ps 9:9 H3068	g.	Ps 37:24 H3068
c.	Ps 143:9 H3068	h.	Ps 9:10 H3068
d.	Ps 37:39 H3068	i.	Ps 145:18 H3068
e.	Ps 37:40 H3068		

Prayer for Helping Others

Heavenly Father even if I am rich in this world, let me be not high minded, nor trust in uncertain riches, but in You the living Theos the Godhead Trinity[a], who gives me richly all things to enjoy;[1] Let me do good, that I may be rich in good works, ready to distribute, willing to communicate;[2] Laying up in store for myself a good foundation against the time to come, that I may lay hold on eternal life.[3] I withhold not good from them to whom it is due, when it is in the power of my hand to do it.[4] Let me not say unto my neighbor, Go, and come again, and tomorrow I will give; when I have it by me[5].

What does it profit, my brethren, though I say I have faith, and have not works? can faith save him?[6] If a brother or sister be naked, and destitute of daily food,[7] Let me not say unto them, Depart in peace, be warmed and filled; not withstanding and I give them not those things which are needful to the body; what does it profit?[8] Even so my faith, if it has not works, is dead, being alone.[9] I give unto the poor and shall not lack: but if I hide my eyes I shall have many a curse.[10] I will be kind and will have blessing, for I give of my bread to the poor.[11] When I show kindness[b] upon the poor I am lending unto You the Self Exisent Eternal Jehovah[c]; and that which I have given will You pay me again.[12]

I give, and it shall be given unto me; good measure, pressed down, and shaken together, and running over, shall men give into my bosom. For with the same measure that I mete with all it shall be measured to me again.[13] I cover and seal the prayer with the Blood of Jesus. In His Name Amen.

Scripture References

1. 1Tim 6:17 KJV   2. 1Tim 6:18 KJV

3.	1Tim 6:19 KJV	9.	Jas 2:17 KJV
4.	Prov 3:27 KJV	10.	Prov 28:27 KJV
5.	Prov 3:28 KJV	11.	Prov 22:9 BBE
6.	Jas 2:14 KJV	12.	Prov 19:17 KJV
7.	Jas 2:15 KJV	13.	Luke 6:38 KJV
8.	Jas 2:16 KJV		

Strong's and Thayer's References

| a. | 1Tim 6:17 G2316 | c. | Prov 19:17 H3068 |
| b. | Prov 19:17 H2603 | | |

Prayer for Hope

You the Self Existent Eternal Jehovah[a] are my portion, says my soul; therefore will I hope in You.[1] You the Self Existent Eternal Jehovah[b] are good unto them that wait for You, to the soul that seeks You.[2]

It is good that I should both hope and quietly wait for the salvation of You the Self Existent Eternal Jehovah[c].[3] I put away fear and let my heart be strong, because I hope in You the Self Existent Eternal Jehovah[d].[4]

See, the eye of You the Self Existent Eternal Jehovah[e] is on those in whose hearts is the fear of You, on those whose hope is in Your mercy;[5] To keep their souls from death; and to keep them living in time of need.[6] My soul is waiting for You the Self Existent Eternal Jehovah[f]; Your my help and my salvation.[7]

For in You my heart has joy; in Your Holy Name is my hope.[8] Let Your mercy be on me, O Self Existent Eternal Jehovah[g], as I am waiting for You.[9]

You are my hiding place and my shield: I hope in Your Word.[10] Uphold me according to Your Word, that I may live: and let me not be ashamed of my hope[11] I wait for You the Self Existent Eternal Jehovah[h], my soul does wait, and in Your Word do I hope.[12] For in You, O Self Existent Eternal Jehovah[i], do I hope: You will hear, O Adonoy[j] my Eloheem[k].[13]

Therefore being justified by faith, I have peace with You Theos the Godhead Trinity[l] through my Kurios the Master[m], Jesus the Anointed Messiah[n]:[14]

By whom also I have access by faith into this grace wherein I stand, and rejoice in hope of the glory of You Theos the Godhead Trinity[o].[15]

Now You Theos the Godhead Trinity[p] *of hope please fill me with all joy and peace in believing, that I may abound in hope, through the power of the Holy Ghost.*[16] *I cover and seal this prayer with the Blood of Jesus. In His Name Amen.*

Scripture References

1.	Lam 3:24 KJV	9.	Ps 33:22 BBE
2.	Lam 3:25 KJV	10.	Ps 119:114 KJV
3.	Lam 3:26KJV	11.	Ps 119:116KJV
4.	Ps 31:24 BBE	12.	Ps 130:5 KJV
5.	Ps 33:18 BBE	13.	Ps 38:15 KJV
6.	Ps 33:19 BBE	14.	Rom 5:1 KJV
7.	Ps 33:20 BBE	15.	Rom 5:2 KJV
8.	Ps 33:21 BBE	16.	Rom 15:13 KJV

Strong's and Thayer's References

a.	Lam 3:24 H3068	i.	Ps 38:15 H3068
b.	Lam 3:25 H3068	j.	Ps 38:15 H136
c.	Lam 3:26 H3068	k.	Ps 38:15 H430
d.	Ps 31:24 H3068	l.	Rom 5:1 G2316
e.	Ps 33:18 H3068	m.	Rom 5:1 G2962
f.	Ps 33:20 H3068	n.	Rom 5:1 G5547
g.	Ps 33:22 H3068	o.	Rom 5:2 G2316
h.	Ps 130:5 H3068	p.	Rom 15:13 G2316

Prayer for Joy

Heavenly Father I have set You the Self Existent Eternal Jehovah[a] always before me: because You are at my right hand, I shall not be moved.[1] Therefore my heart is glad, and my glory rejoices: my flesh also shall rest in hope.[2] You will show me the path of life: in Your presence is fullness of joy; at Your right hand there are pleasures for evermore.[3] Glory and honor are in Your presence; strength and gladness are in Your place.[4] And my soul shall be joyful in You the Self Existent Eternal Jehovah[b]: it shall rejoice in Your salvation.[5]

I will be glad and rejoice in You: I will sing praise to Your name, O thou most High.[6] My soul will be comforted, as with good food; and my mouth will give You praise with songs of joy;[7] When the memory of You comes to me on my bed, and when I give thought to You in the night-time.[8] Because You have been my help, therefore in the shadow of Your wings will I rejoice.[9]

As for me, I will behold Your face in righteousness: I shall be satisfied, when I awake, with Your likeness.[10] The statutes of You the Self Existent Eternal Jehovah[c] are right, rejoicing the heart: the commandment of You the Self Existent Eternal Jehovah[d] is pure, enlightening my eyes.[11] For You have made me most blessed forever: You have made me exceeding   glad   with   Your countenance.[12]

So let all those that put their trust in You rejoice: let them ever shout for joy, because You defend them: let them also that love Your name be joyful in You.[13] You Lord are my strength and my shield; my heart trusted in You, and I am helped:

therefore my heart greatly rejoices; and with my song will I praise You.[14]

Happy is he who has forgiveness for his wrong doing, and whose sin is covered.[15] *Happy is the man in whom You the Self Existent Eternal Jehovah*[e] *sees no evil, and in whose spirit there is no deceit.*[16] *Be glad in the Self Existent Eternal Jehovah*[f] *with joy, you upright men; give cries of joy, all you whose hearts are true.*[17] *By You my sorrow is turned into dancing; You have taken away my clothing of grief, and given me robes of joy;*[18] *So that my glory may make songs of praise to You and not be quiet. O Self Existent Eternal Jehovah*[g] *my Eloheem*[h]*, I will give You praise forever.*[19]

Restore to me the joy of Your salvation. Uphold me with a willing spirit.[20] *That I may show forth all Your praise in the gates of the daughter of Zion: I will rejoice in*

Your salvation.[21] For my heart shall rejoice in You, because I have trusted in Your holy name.[22]

Like those who are looking for You I will be glad and have joy in You; let me and the lovers of Your salvation ever say, May You the Self Existent Eternal Jehovah[i] be great.[23] I cover and seal this prayer with the Blood of Jesus. In His Name Amen.

Scripture References

1.	Ps 16:8 KJV	13.	Ps 5:11 KJV
2.	Ps 16:9 KJV	14.	Ps 28:7 KJV
3.	Ps 16:11 KJV	15.	Ps 32:1 BBE
4.	1Chr 16:27 KJV	16.	Ps 32:2 BBE
5.	Ps 35:9 KJV	17.	Ps 32:11 BBE
6.	Ps 9:2 KJV	18.	Ps 30:11 BBE
7.	Ps 63:5 BBE	19.	Ps 30:12 BBE
8.	Ps 63:6 BBE	20.	Ps 51:12 WEB
9.	Ps 63:7 KJV	21.	Ps 9:14 KJV
10.	Ps 17:15 KJV	22.	Ps 33:21 KJV
11.	Ps 19:8 KJV	23.	Ps 40:16 BBE
12.	Ps 21:6 KJV		

Strong's and Thayer's references

a.	Ps 16:8 H3068	f.	Ps 32:2 H3068
b.	Ps 35:9 H3068	g.	Ps 32:11 H3068
c.	Ps 19:8 H3068	h.	Ps 30:12 H3068
d.	Ps 19:8 H3068	i.	Ps 30:12 H430
e.	Ps 28:7 H3068	j.	Ps 40:16 H3068

Prayer Over Oppression

Father in heaven hear my prayer, O Eloheem[a]; give ear to the words of my mouth.[1] For strangers are risen up against me, and oppressors seek after my soul: they have not set You Eloheem[b] before them. Selah.[2] Attend unto me, and hear me: I mourn in my complaint, and make a noise;[3] Because of the voice of the enemy, because of the oppression of the wicked: for they cast iniquity upon me, and in wrath they hate me.[4]

Keep me as the apple of Your eye, hide me under the shadow of Your wings,[5] From the wicked that oppress me, from my deadly enemies, who compass me about.[6]

You the Self Existent Eternal Jehovah[c] will also be a refuge if I am oppressed, a refuge in times of trouble.[7] And because I know Your name I will put my trust in You: for You the Self Existent Eternal

Jehovah[d], have not forsaken me that seeks You.[8]

Happy am I that has You El the Almighty[e] of Jacob for my help, whose hope is in You the Self Existent Eternal Jehovah[f] my Eloheem[g]:[9] Which made heaven, and earth, the sea, and all that therein is: which keeps truth forever:[10] Which executes judgment for the oppressed: which gives food to the hungry.

You the Self Existent Eternal Jehovah[h] loose the prisoners:[11] I have done what is just and righteous. Don't leave me to my oppressors.[12] Ensure your servant's well-being.

Don't let the proud oppress me.[13] Redeem me from the oppression of man, so I will observe your precepts.[14] You the Self Existent Eternal Jehovah[i] executes righteousness and judgment for all that are oppressed.[15] In righteousness

I shall be established: I shall be far from oppression; for I shall not fear: and from terror; for it shall not come near me.[16] *I cover and seal this prayer with the Blood of Jesus. In His Name Amen.*

Scripture References

1.	Ps 54:2 KJV	9.	Ps 146:5 KJV
2.	Ps 54:3 KJV	10.	Ps 146:6 KJV
3.	Ps 55:2 KJV	11.	Ps 146:7 KJV
4.	Ps 55:3 KJV	12.	Ps 119:121 WEB
5.	Ps 17:8 KJV	13.	Ps 119:122 WEB
6.	Ps 17:9 KJV	14.	Ps 119:134 WEB
7.	Ps 9:9 KJV	15.	Ps 103:6 KJV
8.	Ps 9:10 KJV	16.	Isa 54:14 KJV

Strong's and Thayer's References

a.	Ps 54:2 H430	f.	Ps 146:5 H3068
b.	Ps 54:3 H430	g.	Ps 146:5 H430
c.	Ps 9:9 H3068	h.	Ps 146:7 H3068
d.	Ps 9:10 H3068	i.	Ps 103:6 H3068
e.	Ps 146:5 H410		

Prayer for Overcoming Temptation

Abba I watch and pray, that I enter not into temptation: the spirit indeed is willing, but the flesh is weak.[1] And forgive me my sins; for I also forgive every one that is indebted to me. And lead me not into temptation; but deliver me from evil.[2] Blessed am I that endures temptation: for when I am tried, I shall receive the crown of life, which You Kurios the Master[a] hath promised to me that loves You.[3] You Kurios the Master[b] know how to deliver the godly out of temptations, and to reserve the unjust unto the day of judgment to be punished.[4]

There has no temptation taken me but such as is common to man: but You Theos the Godhead Trinity[c] are faithful, You who will not suffer me to be tempted above that I am able; but will with the temptation also make a way to escape, that I may be able to bear it.⁵ For in that You Yourself have suffered being tempted, You are able to help me who is tempted.⁶

For I have not an high priest which cannot be touched with the feeling of my infirmities; but was in all points tempted like as I am, yet without sin.⁷ Let me therefore come boldly unto Your throne of grace, that I may obtain mercy, and find grace to help in time of need.⁸ And I count it all joy, with my brothers, when I fall into various temptations,⁹ knowing that the testing of my faith produces endurance.¹⁰

Let endurance have its perfect work, that I may be perfect and complete, lacking in nothing.¹¹ Wherein I greatly rejoice, though now for a little while, if need be, I have been put to grief in various trials,¹² that the proof of my faith, which is more precious than gold that perishes even though it is tested by fire, may be found to result in praise, glory, and honor at the revelation of You Jesus the Anointed Messiah[d13] whom not having known I love; in whom, though now I don't see You, yet believing, I rejoice greatly with joy unspeakable and full of glory[14] Because I have kept the word of Your patience, You also will keep me from the hour of temptation, which shall come upon all the world, to try them that dwell upon the earth.[15] I cover and seal this prayer with the Blood of Jesus. In His Name Amen.

Scripture References

1.	Matt 26:41 KJV	9.	Jas 1:2 WEB
2.	Luke 11:4 KJV	10.	Jas 1:3 WEB
3.	Jas 1:12 KJV	11.	Jas 1:4 WEB
4.	2Pet 2:9 KJV	12.	1Pet 1:6 WEB
5.	1Cor 10:13 KJV	13.	1Pet 1:7 WEB
6.	Heb 2:18 WEB	14.	1Pet 1:8 WEB
7.	Heb 4:15 KJV	15.	Rev 3:10 KJV
8.	Heb 4:16 KJV		

Strong's and Thayer's References

a.	Jas 1:12 G2962	c.	1Cor 10:13 G2316
b.	2Pet 2:9 G2962	d.	1Pet 1:7 G5547

Parental Abandonment

Heavenly Father I Cast all my care upon You; for You care for me.[1] When my natural father and my mother forsake me, then You the Self Existent Eternal Jehovah[a] will take me up.[2] And will be a Father unto me, and I shall be a son or daughter, says You the Almighty Kurios the Master[b].[3] You are a father of the fatherless, and a judge of the widows, You are Eloheem[c] in Your Holy Habitation.[4]

You Eloheem[d] set the solitary in families: You bring out those which are bound with chains: but the rebellious dwell in a dry land.[5] You heal my broken heart, and bind up my wounds.[6] And Jesus has prayed to You the Father, and You shall give me another Comforter, that He may abide with me forever;[7] Even the Spirit of truth; whom the world cannot receive, because it sees Him not, neither knows Him: but I know Him; for He dwells with me, and shall be in me.[8]

You will not leave me comfortless You will come to me.[9] I thank You Abba that I am not alone and I cover and seal this prayer with the Blood of Jesus. In His Name Amen.

Scriptures References

1. 1Pet 5:7 KJV
2. Ps 27:10 KJV
3. 2 Cor 6:18 KJV
4. Ps 68:5 KJV
5. Ps 68:6 KJV
6. Ps 147:3 KJV
7. John 14:16 KJV
8. John 14:17 KJV
9. John 14:18 KJV

Strong's and Thayer's References

a. Ps 27:10 H3068
b. 2 Cor 6:18 G2962
c. Ps 68:5 H430
d. Ps 68:6 H430

Perseverance in Prayer

Father in heaven it is written that I should have no cares; but in everything with prayer and praise put my requests before You Theos the Godhead Trinity[a].[1] And Jesus spoke a parable unto us to this end, that we ought always to pray, and not to faint;[2]

And whenever I make a prayer, let there be forgiveness in my heart, if I have anything against anyone; so that I may have forgiveness for my sins from You my Father who is in heaven.[3]

Hearken unto the voice of my cry, my King, and my Eloheem[b]: for unto thee will I pray.[4] Rejoicing in hope; patient in tribulation; continuing instant in prayer;[5]

Before the sun is up, my cry for help comes to Your ear; my hope is in Your Words.[6] My voice shall You hear in the morning, O Self Existent Eternal Jehovah[c]; in the morning will I direct my prayer unto You, and will look up.[7] And in the morning, I rise up a great while before day, and go into a solitary place, and there pray.[8] Evening, and morning, and at noon, will I pray, and cry aloud: and You shall hear my voice.[9] At midnight I will rise to give thanks unto You because of Your righteous judgments.[10]

And like as Timothy has exhorted I first of all will make supplications, prayers, intercessions, and giving of thanks, for all men;[11] For kings, and for all that are in authority; that I may lead a quiet and peaceable life in all godliness and honesty.[12] Praying always with all prayer and supplication in the Spirit, and watching with all perseverance and supplication for all saints;[13]

I give myself to prayer at all times, keeping watch with praise;[14] And pray without ceasing.[15] O come, let me worship and bow down: let me kneel before You the Self Existent Eternal Jehovah[d] my maker.[16] I cover and seal this prayer with the Blood of Jesus. In His Name Amen.

Scripture References

1.	Phil 4:6 BBE	9.	Ps 55:17 KJV
2.	Luke 18:1 KJV	10.	Ps 119:62 KJV
3.	Mark 11:25 BBE	11.	1Tim 2:1 KJV
4.	Ps 5:2 KJV	12.	1Tim 2:2 KJV
5.	Rom 12:12 KJV	13.	Eph 6:18 KJV
6.	Ps 119:147 BBE	14.	Col 4:2 BBE
7.	Ps 5:3 KJV	15.	1Thess 5:17 KJV
8.	Mark 1:35 KJV	16.	Ps 95:6 KJV

Strong's and Thayer's References

a.	Phil 4:6 G2316	c.	Ps 5:3 H3068
b.	Ps 5:2 H430	d.	Ps 95:6 H3068

Prayer for Praise

O Adonoy[a], open my lips; and my mouth shall show forth Your praise.[1] And my tongue shall speak of Your righteousness and of Your praise all day long.[2] Because Your loving kindness is better than life, my lips shall praise You.[3]

Let my mouth be filled with Your praise and with Your honor all day.[4] I will greatly praise You with my mouth the Self Existent Eternal Jehovah[b]; yes, I will praise You among the multitude.[5]

I Enter into Your gates with thanksgiving, and into Your courts with praise: I am thankful unto You, and bless Your name.[6] For You the Self Existent Eternal Jehovah[c] are good; Your mercy is everlasting; and Your truth endures to all generations.[7]

Praise You Jah, the Lord, most Vehement[d]. Praise, O you servants of the Self Existent Eternal Jehovah[e], praise the name of the Self Existent Eternal Jehovah[f].[8] Blessed be Your name Self Existent Eternal Jehovah[g] from this time forth and for evermore.[9] From the rising of the sun unto the going down of the same, You the Self Existent Eternal Jehovah's[h] name is to be praised.[10]

Seven times a day do I give You praise, because of Your upright decisions.[11] In You Eloheem[i] I boast all the day long, and praise Your name forever. Selah.[12]

For You the Self Existent Eternal Jehovah[j] are great, and greatly to be praised: You are to be feared above all gods.[13] For all the gods of the nations are idols: but You the Self Existent Eternal Jehovah[k] made the heavens.[14]

Honor and majesty are before You: strength and beauty are in Your sanctuary.[15] *For great are You the Self Existent Eternal Jehovah*[l], *and greatly to be praised: You also are to be feared above all gods.*[16] *For all the gods of the people are idols: but You the Self Existent Eternal Jehovah*[m] *made the heavens.*[17]

Glory and honor are in Your presence; strength and gladness are in Your place.[18] *You are my Eloheem*[n], *and I will praise You: You are my Eloheem*[o], *I will exalt You.*[19] *I give thanks unto You the Self Existent Eternal Jehovah*[p]; *for You are good: for Your mercy endures forever.*[20] *So I a person and sheep of Your pasture will give You thanks for ever: I will show forth Your praise to all generations.*[21] *I will give You thanks in the great congregation: I will praise You among much people.*[22]

Oh that men would praise You the Self Existent Eternal Jehovah[q] for Your goodness, and for Your wonderful works to the children of men![23] According to Your name, O Eloheem[r], so is Your praise unto the ends of the earth: Your right hand is full of righteousness.[24]

I will praise You, O Adonoy[s] my Eloheem[t], with all my heart: and I will glorify Your name for evermore.[25] I cover and seal this prayer with the Blood of Jesus. In His Name Amen.

Scripture References

1.	Ps 51:15 KJV	14.	Ps 96:5 KJV
2.	Ps 35:28 KJV	15.	Ps 96:6 KJV
3.	Ps 63:3 KJV	16.	1Chr 16:25 KJV
4.	Ps 71:8 KJV	17.	1Chr 16:26 KJV
5.	Ps 109:30 KJV	18.	1Chr 16:27 KJV
6.	Ps 100:4 KJV	19.	Ps 118:28 KJV
7.	Ps 100:5 KJV	20.	Ps 118:29 KJV
8.	Ps 113:1 KJV	21.	Ps 79:13 KJV
9.	Ps 113:2 KJV	22.	Ps 35:18 KJV
10.	Ps 113:3 KJV	23.	Ps 107:8 KJV
11.	Ps 119:164 BBE	24.	Ps 48:10 KJV
12.	Ps 44:8 KJV	25.	Ps 86:12 KJV
13.	Ps 96:4 KJV		

Strong's and Thayer's References

a.   Ps 51:15 H136
b.   Ps 109:30 H3068
c.   Ps 100:5 H3068
d.   Ps 113:1 H3050
e.   Ps 113:1 H3068
f.   Ps 113:1 H3068
g.   Ps 113:2 H3068
h.   Ps 113:3 H3068
i.   Ps 44:8 H430
j.   Ps 96:4 H3068

k.   Ps 96:5 H3068
l.   1Chr 16:25 H3068
m.   1Chr 16:26 H3068
n.   Ps 118:28 H430
o.   Ps 118:28 H430
p.   Ps 118:29 H3068
q.   Ps 107:8 H3068
r.   Ps 48:10 H430
s.   Ps 86:12 H136
t.   Ps 86:12 H430

Prodigals Return to the Lord

Father in heaven You say If Your people, which are called by Your name, shall humble themselves, and pray, and seek Your face, and turn from their wicked ways; then You will hear from heaven, and will forgive their sin, and will heal their land.[1] When they are in tribulation, and all these things are come upon them, even in the latter days, if they turn to You the Self Existent Eternal Jehovah[a] Eloheem[b], and shalt be obedient unto Your voice;[2] (For You the Self Existent Eternal Jehovah[c] Eloheem[d] are a merciful El the Almighty[e];) You will not forsake them, neither destroy them, or forget the covenant of their fathers which You sware unto them.[3]

Have You any pleasure at all that the wicked should die? says You Adonoy[f] Yehhovee[g]: and not that they should return from their ways, and live?[4] For You have no pleasure in the death of them that die, says You Adonoy[h] Yehhovee[i]: wherefore let them turn their selves, and live.[5]

Let them repent therefore, and be converted, that their sins may be blotted out, when the times of refreshing shall come from the presence of You Kurios the Master[j].[6] You Kurios the Master[k] are not slack concerning Your promise, as some men count slackness; but is longsuffering to us-ward, not willing that any should perish, but that all should come to repentance.[7]

And You will cleanse them from all their iniquity, whereby they have sinned against You; and You will pardon all their iniquities, whereby they have sinned, and whereby they have transgressed against You.[8]

Come near to Theos the Godhead Trinity[l] and He will come near to you. Make your hands clean, you evil-doers; put away deceit from your hearts, you false in mind.[9] Therefore say I unto them, Thus says the Self Existent Eternal Jehovah[m] of hosts; Turn unto Him, says the Self Existent Eternal Jehovah[n] of hosts, and He will turn unto you, says the Self Existent Eternal Jehovah[o] of hosts.[10] Return, you backsliding children, and He will heal your backslidings. Behold, let them come unto You; for You are the Self Existent Eternal Jehovah[p] their Eloheem[q].[11] You will heal their backsliding, You will love them freely: for Your anger is turned away from them.[12] You, even You, are He that blots out their transgressions for their own sake, and will not remember their sins.[13]

So turn, O backsliding children, says Self Existent Eternal Jehovah[r]; for He is married to you: and He will take you one of a city, and two of a family, and He will bring you to

Zion:[14] As far as the east is from the west, so far has He removed our transgressions from us.[15]

Therefore the redeemed of the self Existent Eternal Jehovah[s] shall return, and come with singing unto Zion; and everlasting joy shall be upon their head: they shall obtain gladness and joy; and sorrow and mourning shall flee away.[16] And He will give them pastors according to His heart, which shall feed them with knowledge and understanding.[17] And it is appropriate to celebrate and be glad, for this, because our brother, was dead, and is alive again. He was lost, and is found.[8] And they shall be His people, and He will be their Eloheem[t].[19] I cover and seal this prayer with the Blood of Jesus. In His Name Amen.

Scripture References

1.	2Chr 7:14 KJV	3.	Deut 4:31 KJV
2.	Deut 4:30 KJV	4.	Ezek 18:23 KJV

5.	Ezek 18:32 KJV	13.	Isa 43:25 KJV
6.	Acts 3:19 KJV	14.	Jer 3:14 KJV
7.	2Pet 3:9 KJV	15.	Ps 103:12 KJV
8.	Jer 33:8 KJV	16.	Isa 51:11 KJV
9.	Jas 4:8 BBE	17.	Jer 3:15 KJV
10.	Zech 1:3 KJV	18.	Luke 15:32 WEB
11.	Jer 3:22 KJV	19.	Jer 30:22 KJV
12.	Hos 14:4 KJV		

Strong's and Thayer's References

a.	Deut 4:30 H3068	l.	Jas 4:8 G2316
b.	Duet 4:30 H430	m.	Zech 1:3 H3068
c.	Deut 4:31 H3068	n.	Zech 1:3 H3068
d.	Duet 4:31 H430	o.	Zech 1:3 H3068
e.	Duet 4:31 H410	p.	Jer 3:22 H3068
f.	Ezek 18:23 H136	q.	Jer 3:22 H430
g.	Ezek 18:23 H3069	r.	Jer 3:14 H3068
h.	Ezek 18:32 H136	s.	Isa 51:11 H3068
i.	Ezek 18:32 H3069	t.	Jer 30:22 H430
j.	Acts 3:19 G2962		
k.	2Pet 3:9 G2962		

Prayer for Provision

Heavenly Father, I cast all my care on You because You care and provide for me.[1] And I say like Moses, that the people bring much more than enough for the service of the work, which You Jehovah the Existing One[a] commanded to make.[2]

Therefore I take no thought, saying, What shall I eat? or, What shall I drink? or, What shall I be clothed with?[3] And I seek not what I shall eat, or what I shall drink, and I do not have a doubtful mind.[4] For I know that others seek after all these things but I trust You my heavenly Father because You know that I have need of all these things.[5]

But I seek first Your Kingdom Theos the Godhead Trinity[b], and Your Righteousness; and all these things are added unto me.[6] And You Theos the Godhead Trinity[c] are able to make all grace abound toward me;

that I, always having all sufficiency in all things, may abound to every good work:[7] *As it is written, You have dispersed abroad; You have taken care of those in need: Your righteousness remains forever.*[8] *Now You that ministers seed to the sower does both minister bread for my food, and multiply my seed sown, and increase the fruits of my righteousness.*[9] *Being enriched in everything to all bountifulness, which causes thanksgiving to You Theos the Godhead Trinity*[d].[10]

I have decreed this in the Name of Jesus and it shall be established and the light shall shine upon my ways.[11] *I cover and seal this prayer with the Blood of Jesus. In His Name Amen.*

Scripture References

1. 1Pet 5:7 KJV
2. Exod 36:5 KJV
3. Matt 6:31 KJV
4. Luke 12:29 KJV
5. Matt 6:32 KJV
6. Matt 6:33 KJV
7. 2 Cor 9:8 KJV
8. 2 Cor 9:9 KJV
9. 2 Cor 9:10 KJV
10. 2 Cor 9:11 KJV
11. Job 22:28.KJV

Strong's and Thayer's Reference

a.   Exod 36:5 H3068   c.   2 Cor 9:8 G2316

b.   Matt 6:33 G2316   d.   2 Cor 9:11 G2316

Prayer for Returning Good for Evil

Abba I choose not to render evil for evil unto any man; but ever follow that which is good, both among those I know, and to all men.[1] I have heard that it has been said, I shalt love my neighbor, and hate my enemy.[2] But Jesus says unto me, Love my enemies, bless them that curse me, do good to them that hate me, and pray for them which despitefully use me, and persecute me;[3] That I may be a child of You my Father which is in heaven: for You make Your sun to rise on the evil and on the good, and sends rain on the just and on the unjust.[4]

For if I love them which love me, what reward have I ? do not even the publicans the same?[5] But Jesus says unto me and I listen, to love my enemies, do good to them which hate me,[6] Bless them that curse me, and *pray for them which despitefully use me.*[7] *And unto him that smites me on the one cheek offer also the other; and him that takes away my cloke forbid not to take thy coat also.*[8]

I will not say that I will do so to him as he hath done to me I will not render to the man according to his work[9] *Because I recompense to no man evil for evil. I provide things honest in the sight of all men.*[10] *If it be possible, as much as lies in me, I live peaceably with all men.*[11] *I avenge not myself, but rather give place unto wrath: for it is written, Vengeance is Yours; You will repay, says You Kurios the Master*[a].[12] *Therefore if my enemy hungers, I feed him; if he thirst, I give him drink: for in so doing I shalt heap coals of fire on his head.*[13] *I be not overcome of evil, but overcome evil with good.*[14]

Finally, I will be of one mind, having compassion on others, I love as brethren, I be pitiful, and courteous:[15] *Not rendering evil for evil, or railing for railing: but contrariwise blessing; knowing that I am called, that I should inherit a blessing.*[16] *For me that will love life, and see good days, let me refrain my tongue from evil, and my lips that they speak no guile:*[17] *Let me eschew evil, and do good; let me seek peace, and ensue it.*[18]

For the eyes of You Kurios the Master[b] *are over the righteous, and his ears are open unto their prayers: but the face of You Kurios the Master*[c] *are against them that do evil.*[19] *I will not say, I will recompense evil; but wait on the You Self Existent Eternal Jehovah*[d], *and You shall save me.*[20] *I cover and seal this prayer with the Blood of Jesus. In His Name Amen.*

Scripture References

1.	1Thes 5:15 KJV	11.	Rom 12:18 KJV
2.	Matt 5:43 KJV	12.	Rom 12:19 KJV
3.	Matt 5:44 KJV	13.	Rom 12:20 KJV
4.	Matt 5:45 KJV	14.	Rom 12:21 KJV
5.	Matt 5:46 KJV	15.	1Pet 3:8 KJV
6.	Luke 6:27 KJV	16.	1Pet 3:9 KJV
7.	Luke 6:28 KJV	17.	1Pet 3:10 KJV
8.	Luke 6:29 KJV	18.	1Pet 3:11 KJV
9.	Prov 24:29 KJV	19.	1Pet 3:12 KJV
10.	Rom 12:17 KJV	20.	Prov 20:22 KJV

Strong's and Thayer's References

a.	Rom 12:19 G2962	c.	1Pet 3:12 G2962
b.	1Pet 3:12 G2962	d.	Prov 20:22 H3068

Prayer for Safety

It is written that the name of You Jehovah the Self Existent Eternal[a] is a strong tower: the righteous runs into it, and are safe.[1] The fear of man brings a snare: but he who puts his trust in You Jehovah the Self Existent Eternal[b] shall be safe.[2] I choose to trust in You the Lord and be safe.

But whoever gives ear to You will take his rest safely, living in peace without fear of evil.[3] So I choose to listen to You the Lord and live in peace without fear of evil.

So I keep Your rules and Your decisions and do them, and I will be safe in my land.[4] But when I go over Jordan my new boundary, and dwell in the land which You Jehovah the Self Existent Eternal[c] Eloheem[d] gives me to inherit, and when You give me rest from all my enemies round about, so that I dwell in safety;[5] Then shalt I walk safely, and my foot shall not stumble.⁶

I will both lay me down in peace, and sleep: for You, Jehovah the Self Existent Eternalᵉ, only make me dwell in safety.⁷ But You Kurios the Masterᶠ are faithful, to establish and keep me from evil.⁸

Because I have set my love upon You, therefore You will deliver me: and will set me on high, because I have known Your Name.⁹ And forgive me my sins; for I also forgive every one that is indebted to me. And lead me not into temptation; but deliver me from evil.¹⁰ For Yours is the kingdom, and the power, and the glory, forever. Amen.¹¹

And Jesus prays not that You should take me out of the world, but that You should keep me from the evil.¹²

You Jehovah the Self Existent Eternalᵍ shall preserve me from all

evil: You shall preserve my soul.[13]
And You Kurios the Master[h] *shall deliver me from every evil work, and will preserve me unto Your heavenly kingdom: to whom be glory for ever and ever. Amen.*[14] *I cover and seal this prayer with the Blood of Jesus. In His Name Amen.*

Scripture References

1.	Prov 18:10 KJV	8.	2Thess 3:3 KJV
2.	Prov 29:25 KJV	9.	Ps 91:14 KJV
3.	Prov 1:33 BBE	10.	Luke 11:4 KJV
4.	Lev 25:18 BBE	11.	Matt 6:13 KJV
5.	Deut 12:10 KJV	12.	John 17:15 KJV
6.	Prov 3:23 KJV	13.	Ps 121:7 KJV
7.	Ps 4:8 KJV	14.	2Tim 4:18 KJV

Strong's and Thayer's References

a.	Prov 18:10 H3068	e.	Ps 4:8 H3068
b.	Prov 29:25 H3068	f.	2Thess 3:3 G2962
c.	Deut 12:10 H3068	g.	Ps 121:7 H3068
d.	Deut 12:10 H430	h.	2Tim 4:18 G2962

Prayer to Seek the Lord

Father in Heaven When You said, for me to Seek Your face; my heart said to You, Your face, the Self Existent Eternal Jehovah[a], will I seek.[1] Glory in Your holy name: let my heart rejoice that I seek You the Self Existent Eternal Jehovah[b].[2] I seek You the Self Existent Eternal Jehovah[c] and Your strength, seek Your face continually.[3]

I seek You the Self Existent Eternal Jehovah[d] while You may be found, I call upon You while You are near.[4] Therefore You say unto me, You the Self Existent Eternal Jehovah[e] of hosts says; to turn unto You, says You the Self Existent Eternal Jehovah[f] of hosts, and You will turn unto me, says You the Self Existent Eternal Jehovah[g] of hosts.[5]

Therefore I turn to You Eloheem[h]: keep mercy and judgment, and wait on You Eloheem[i] continually.[6] You

121

love me that loves You; and those that seek You early shall find You.[7]

For You the Self Existent Eternal Jehovah[j] say unto the house of Israel, to seek You, and they shall live:[8] And You have made of one blood all nations of men for to dwell on all the face of the earth, and have determined the times before appointed, and the bounds of their habitation;[9] That they should seek You Kurios the Master[k], if haply they might feel after You, and find You, though You be not far from every one of us:[10]

The humble shall see this, and be glad: and hearts shall live that seek You Eloheem[l].[11]

Let all those that seek You rejoice and be glad in You: and let such as love Your salvation say continually, Let You Eloheem[m] be magnified.[12] I glory in Your Holy Name: let my *heart rejoice that I seek You the Self Existent Eternal Jehovah[n].[13]*

I seek You the Self Existent Eternal Jehovah[o], and Your strength: I seek Your face evermore.[14] I cover and seal this prayer with the Blood of Jesus. In His Name Amen.

Scripture References

1.	Ps 27:8 KJV	8.	Amos 5:4 KJV
2.	1Chr 16:10 KJV	9.	Acts 17:26 KJV
3.	1Chr 16:11 KJV	10.	Acts 17:27 KJV
4.	Isa 55:6 KJV	11.	Ps 69:32 KJV
5.	Zech 1:3 KJV	12.	Ps 70:4 KJV
6.	Hos 12:6 KJV	13.	Ps 105:3 KJV
7.	Prov 8:17 KJV	14.	Ps 105:4 KJV

Strong's and Thayer's References

a.	Ps 27:8 H3068	i.	Hos 12:6 H430
b.	1Chr 16:10 H3068	j.	Amos 5:4 H3068
c.	1Chr 16:11 H3068	k.	Acts 17:27 G2962
d.	Isa 55:6 H3068	l.	Ps 69:32 H430
e.	Zech 1:3 H3068	m.	Ps 70:4 H430
f.	Zech 1:3 H3068	n.	Ps 105:3 H3068
g.	Zech 1:3 H3068	o.	Ps 105:4 H3068
h.	Hos 12:6 H430		

Prayer for Sleep

Abba, I thank You that Your Word says that I will both lay me down in peace, and sleep: because only You the Self Existent Eternal Jehovah[a], makes me to dwell in safety.[1] It is vain for me to rise up early, to sit up late, to meditate on thoughts of sorrows: so You give Your beloved sleep.[2] And I am one of Your beloveds.[3] When I take my rest I will have no fear, and on my bed, my sleep will be sweet.[4] I will lay me down and sleep; and upon awakening; I will see that You the Self Existent Eternal Jehovah[b] sustained me.[5] I cover and seal this prayer with the Blood of Jesus. In His Name Amen.

Scripture References

1.	Ps 4:8 KJV	4.	Prov 3:24 BBE
2.	Ps 127:2 KJV	5.	Ps 3:5 KJV
3.	Song 6:3 KJV		

Strong's and Thayer's References

a.	Ps 4:8 H3068	b.	Ps 3:5 H3068

Prayer for Souls

Abba In Jesus Name and through His Blood I come boldly unto Your throne of grace, that I may obtain mercy for lost souls, and find grace to help win them.[1] So shall my word be that goes forth out of my mouth: it shall not return unto me void, but it shall accomplish that which I please, and it shall prosper in the thing it was sent for.[2]

And Bless You the LORD, all His angels, that excel in strength, that do Your commandments hearkening unto the voice of Your Word.[3] Let my prayer come before you, Eloheem[a] and please listen to the words of my mouth.[4] All souls belong to You Lord,[6] in Your hand is the soul of every living thing, and the breath of all people.[5] Help me to be fruitful and receive wisdom to win souls.[7]

Adonoy[b] *Yehhovee*[c] come against those that are hunting souls to make them fly, and tear them from their enemy arms and command the souls to be let go, even the souls that they hunt to make them fly.[8] Tear off their veils and deliver your people out of enemy hands and bind the enemy from hunting them anymore and the enemy shall know that You are the Self Existent, Eternal Jehovah[d].[9] Deliver their soul from the midst of lions; and from among the enemy that is set on fire, the sons of men, whose teeth are spears and arrows, and their tongue a sharp sword.[10]

Take them out of the power of the workers of evil, and keep them safe from men of blood.[11] Deliver them from those that speak against them[12]; and from those that scheme against and lay wait to take and persecute their soul saying, that You *Eloheem*[e] have forsaken him so there is no one

126

to deliver him.[13] For the enemy is watching in secret for their soul; the strong have come together against the innocent, O Jehovah Eternal; rescue them.[14] Lose them from deception and divination and deliver them out of the hands of the enemy, and they shall know that You are Jehovah Eternal, the Self Existent[g] One.[15] Deliver them from the evil that is after their soul to crush their life in darkness like those who are dead.[16] Have mercy on them whose spirit is overcome and bring peace to their fearful hearts.[17]

Praise be to You Eternal Jehovah[h], who saves them from being wounded by the teeth of the enemy.[18] Draw near unto their soul and redeem them from their enemies.[19]

You Kurios the Master[i] are not slack concerning Your promise, as some men count slackness; but are longsuffering to us-ward, not willing *that any should perish, but that all should come to repentance.*[20]

Eternal Jehovah[j] *You the maker of heaven and earth, the authority of Your Name is their help.*[21] *Eloheem*[k]*, be not far from them, O Eloheem*[l] *make haste to help them.*[22] *Please keep them safe from all evil and take care of their soul as You have promised, Jehovah the Self Existent Eternal*[m]*.*[23] *Praise You Jah, the Lord, most Vehement*[n]*, Praise You the Eternal Jehovah*[o]*, O my Soul!*[24] *I cover and seal this prayer with the Blood of Jesus. In His Name Amen.*

Scripture References

1.	Heb 4:16 KJV	13.	Ps 71:11 KJV
2.	Isa 55:11 KJV	14.	Ps 59:3 BBE
3.	Ps 103:20 KJV	15.	Eze 13:23 KJV
4.	Ps 54:2 BBE	16.	Ps 143:3 BBE
5.	Eze 18:4 BBE	17.	Ps 143:4 BBE
6.	Job 12:10 KJV	18.	Ps 124:6 BBE
7.	Prov 11:30 KJV	19.	Ps 69:18 KJV
8.	Eze 13:20 KJV	20.	2Pe 3:9 KJV
9.	Eze 13:21 KJV	21.	Ps 124:8 BBE
10.	Ps 57:4 KJV	22.	Ps 71:12 KJV
11.	Ps 59:2 BBE	23.	Ps 121:7 BBE
12.	Ps 71:10 KJV	24.	Ps 146:1 KJV

Strong's and Thayer's References

a.	Ps 54:2 H430	i.	2Pe 3:9 G2962
b.	Eze 13:20 H136	j.	Ps 124:8 H3068
c.	Eze 13:20 H3069	k.	Ps 71:12 H430
d.	Eze 13:21 H3068	l.	Ps 71:12 H430
e.	Ps 71:11 H430	m.	Ps 121:7 H3O68
f.	Ps 59:3 H3068	n.	Ps 146:1 H3050
g.	Eze 13:23 H3068	o.	Ps 146:1 H3068
h.	Ps 124:6 H3068		

Prayer for Strength

Heavenly Father if my soul is weary with sorrow: strengthen me according to your Word.[1] Also please grant me, according to the riches of Your glory, to be strengthened with might by Your Spirit in my inner man.[2] You give power to the faint; and to them that have no might You increase strength.[3]

And they that wait upon You Jehovah the Self Existent Eternal One[a] shall renew their strength; they shall mount up with wings as eagles; they shall run, and not be weary; and they shall walk, and not faint.[4]

I wait on You Jehovah the Self Existent Eternal One[b]: be of good courage, and You shall strengthen my heart: wait, I say, on You Jehovah, the Self Existent Eternal One[c].[5] I choose to wait on You. It is You El the Almighty[d] that girds me with strength, and makes my way *perfect.*[6] *You make my feet like hinds' feet, and sets me upon my high places.*[7] *You teach my hands to war, so that a bow of steel is broken by mine arms.*[8] *I have no fear, for You are with me; do not be looking about in trouble, for You are my Eloheem*[e]*; You will give me strength, yes, You will be my helper; yes, Your true right hand will be my support.*[9]

You have also given me the shield of Your salvation. Your right hand sustains me. Your gentleness has made me great.[10] *You Jehovah the Self Existent Eternal One*[f] *will give strength unto me one of Your people; You Jehovah the Self Existent Eternal One*[g] *will bless me one of Your people with peace.*[11]

When my cry came to Your ears You gave me an answer, and made me great with strength in my soul.[12]

You Jehovah the Self Existent Eternal One[h] *are my strength and*

*my shield; my heart trusts in You,
and I am helped: therefore my heart
greatly rejoices; and with my song
will I praise You.*[13] *I cover and seal
this prayer with the Blood of Jesus.
In His Name Amen.*

Scripture References

1. Ps 119:28 WEB
2. Eph 3:16 KJV
3. Isa 40:29 KJV
4. Isa 40:31 KJV
5. Ps 27:14 KJV
6. Ps 18:32 KJV
7. Ps 18:33 KJV
8. Ps 18:34 KJV
9. Isa 41:10 BBE
10. Ps 18:35 WEB
11. Ps 29:11 KJV
12. Ps 138:3 BBE
13. Ps 28:7 KJV

Strong's and Thayer's References

a. Isa 40 :31 H3068
b. Ps 27:14 H3068
c. Ps 27:14 H3068
d. Ps 18:32 H410
e. Isa 41:10 H430
f. Ps 29:11 H3068
g. Ps 29:11 H3068
h. Ps 28:7 H3068

Prayer for Thanksgiving to God

Father in Heaven I enter into Your gates with thanksgiving, and into Your courts with praise: be thankful unto You, and bless Your name.[1] O I give thanks unto You the Self Existent Eternal Jehovah[a]; for You are good: because Your mercy endures forever.[2] I Rejoice in You the Self Existent Eternal Jehovah[b], am righteous; and give thanks at the remembrance of Your Holiness[3].

I Praise You Yaw the Lord most Vehement[c]. I give thanks unto You the Self Existent Eternal Jehovah[d]; for You are good: for Your mercy endures forever.[4] I give thanks unto You the Self Existent Eternal Jehovah[e], call upon Your name, make known Your deeds among the people.[5] So I one of Your people and sheep of Your pasture will give You thanks for ever: I will show forth Your praise to all generations.[6]

I will give You thanks in the great congregation: I will praise You among much people.[7] Giving thanks always for all things unto You Theos the Godhead Trinity[f] and Father in the name of my Kurios the Master[g] Jesus the anointed Messiah[h],[8] Let me come before Your presence with thanksgiving, and make a joyful noise unto You with psalms.[9] Therefore will I give thanks unto You, Self Existent Eternal Jehovah[i], among the heathen, and sing praises unto Your name.[10]

O give thanks unto You the Self Existent Eternal Jehovah[j], for You are good: for Your mercy endures forever.[11] O give thanks unto You El the Almighty[k] of heaven: for Your mercy endures forever.[12] At midnight I will rise to give thanks unto You because of Your righteous judgments.[13]

Now thanks be unto You Theos the Godhead Trinity[l], which always causes me to triumph in the anointed Messiah[m], and makes manifest the savour of Your knowledge by me in every place.[14] And whatsoever I do in word or deed, I do all in the name of You Kurios the Master[n], Jehovah Who is Salvation[o], giving thanks to You Theos the Godhead Trinity[p] and the Father by Him.[15] In everything I give thanks: for this is the will of You Theos the Godhead Trinity[q] in the anointed Messiah[r], Jehovah Who is Salvation[s] concerning me.[16]

Now therefore, my Eloheem[t], I thank thee, and praise Your glorious name.[17] I cover and seal this prayer with the Blood of Jesus. In His Name Amen.

Scripture References

1. Ps 100:4 KJV   2.   Ps 118:1 KJV

135

3.	Ps 97:12 KJV	11.	Ps 107:1 KJV
4.	Ps 106:1 KJV	12.	Ps 136:26 KJV
5.	1Chr 16:8 KJV	13.	Ps 119:62 KJV
6.	Ps 79:13 KJV	14.	2Cor 2:14 KJV
7.	Ps 35:18 KJV	15.	Col 3:17 KJV
8.	Eph 5:20 KJV	16.	1Thess 5:18 KJV
9.	Ps 95:2 KJV	17.	1Chr 29:13 KJV
10.	Ps 18:49 KJV		

Strong's and Thayer's References

a.	Ps 118:1 H3068	k.	Ps 136:26 H410
b.	Ps 97:12 H3068	l.	2Cor 2:14 G2316
c.	Ps 106:1 H3050.	m.	2Cor 2:14 G5547
d.	Ps 106:1 H3068	n.	Col 3:17 G2962
e.	1Chr 16:8 H3068	o.	Col 3:17 G2424
f.	Eph 5:20 G2316	p.	Col 3:17 G2316
g.	Eph 5:20 G2962	q.	1Thess 5:18 G2316
h.	Eph 5:20 G5547	r.	1Thess 5:18 G5547
i.	Ps 18:49 H3068	s.	1 Thess 5:18 G2424
j.	Ps 107:1 H3068	t.	1Chr 29:13 H430

Prayer for the Afflicted

I come to You Father with a prayer when I am afflicted, when I am overwhelmed, and pour out my complaint before You the Self Existent Eternal Jehovah[a]. Hear my prayer, O Self Existent Eternal Jehovah[b], and let my cry come unto thee.[1] And when I am in affliction, I beseech You the Self Existent Eternal Jehovah[c] my Eloheem[d], and humble myself greatly before You the Eloheem[e] of my fathers,[2] I pour out my complaint before You. I tell You my troubles.[3]

I cry unto You, O Self Existent Eternal Jehovah[f]: I say, You are my refuge and my portion in the land of the living.[4]

Attend unto my cry; for I am brought very low: deliver me from my persecutors; for they are stronger than I.[5]

When my soul faints within me I remember You the Self Existent Eternal Jehovah[g]: and my prayer comes in unto You, into Your Holy temple.[6] Bring my soul out of prison, that I may praise Your name: the righteous shall compass me about; for You shalt deal bountifully with me.[7] Be merciful unto me, O Adonoy[h]: for I cry unto You daily.[8] I looked unto You, and am lightened: and my face is not ashamed.[9] I am a poor man and cry, and You the Self Existent Eternal Jehovah[i] hear me, and save me out of all my troubles.[10]

You will regard the prayer of the destitute, and not despise my prayer.[11] You the Self Existent Eternal Jehovah[j] are good, a strong hold in the day of trouble; and You know me that trusts in You.[12] You the Self Existent Eternal Jehovah[k] are my rock, and my fortress, and my deliverer; my El the Almighty[l], my strength, in whom I will trust;

my buckler, and the horn of my salvation, and my high tower.[13]

As for me, I will call upon You Eloheem[m]; and You the Self Existent Eternal Jehovah[n] shall save me.[14] *I cover and seal this prayer with the Blood of Jesus. In His Name Amen.*

Scripture References

1. Ps 102:1 KJV
2. 2Chr 33:12 KJV
3. Ps 142:2 WEB
4. Ps 142:5 KJV
5. Ps 142:6 KJV
6. Jonah 2:7 KJV
7. Ps 142:7 KJV
8. Ps 86:3 KJV
9. Ps 34:5 KJV
10. Ps 34:6 KJV
11. Ps 102:17 KJV
12. Nah 1:7 KJV
13. Ps 18:2 KJV
14. Ps 55:16 KJV

Strong's and Thayer's References

a. Ps 102:1 H3068
b. Ps 102:1 H3068
c. 2Chr 33:12 H3068
d. 2Chr 33:12 H430
e. 2Chr 33:12 H430
f. Ps 142:5 H3068
g. Jonah 2:7 H3068
h. Ps 86:3 H136
i. Ps 34:6 H3068
j. Nah 1:7 H3068
k. Ps 18:2 H3068
l. Ps 18:2 H410
m. Ps 55:16 H430
n. Ps 55:16 H3068

Thinking Pleasant Thoughts

Heavenly Father my meditation of You shall be sweet: I will be glad in You the Self Existent Eternal Jehovah[a].[1] I will meditate also of all Your work, and talk of Your doings.[2] Your way, O Eloheem[b], is in the sanctuary: who is so great as El the Almighty[c] as You my Eloheem[d]?[3]

You are El the Almighty[e] that does wonders: You have declared Your strength among the people.[4] I give thanks unto You the Self Existent Eternal Jehovah[f], call upon Your name, make known Your deeds among the people.[5]

I sing unto You, sing psalms unto You, I talk of all Your wondrous works.[6]

I will remember the works of You Yaw the Lord most Vehement[g]: surely I will remember Your wonders of old.[7] Remember Your marvelous works that You have done, Your wonders, and the judgments of Your mouth;[8] You have made Your wonderful works to be remembered: You the Self Existent Eternal Jehovah[h] are gracious and full of compassion.[9]

I set my affection on things above, not on things on the earth.[10] And I be not conformed to this world: but I be transformed by the renewing of my mind, that I may prove what is that good, and acceptable, and perfect, will of You Theos the Godhead Trinity[i].[11]

And herein do I exercise myself, to have always a conscience void of offence toward You Theos the Godhead Trinity[j], and toward men.[12] Let this mind be in me, which was also in You the anointed Messiah[k], Jehovah Who is Salvation[l].[13]

Finally, whatsoever things are true, whatsoever things are honest,

*whatsoever things are just,
whatsoever things are pure,
whatsoever things are lovely,
whatsoever things are of good
report; if there be any virtue, and if
there be any praise, I think on these
things.*[14] *I cover and seal this prayer
with the Blood of Jesus. In His Name
Amen.*

Scripture Reference's

1.	Ps 104:34 KJV
2.	Ps 77:12 KJV
3.	Ps 77:13 KJV
4.	Ps 77:14 KJV
5.	1Chr 16:8 KJV
6.	1Chr 16:9 KJV
7.	Ps 77:11 KJV
8.	1Chr 16:12 KJV
9.	Ps 111:4 KJV
10.	Col 3:2 KJV
11.	Rom 12:2 KJV
12.	Acts 24:16 KJV
13.	Phil 2:5 KJV
14.	Phil 4:8 KJV

Strong's and Thayer's References

a.	Ps 104:34 H3068
b.	Ps 77:13 H430
c.	Ps 77:13 H410
d.	Ps 77:13 H430
e.	Ps 77:14 H410
f.	1Chr 16:8 H3068
g.	Ps 77:11 H3050
h.	Ps 111:4 H3068
i.	Rom 12:2 G2316
j.	Acts 24:16 G2316
k.	Phil 2:5 G5547
l.	Phil 2:5 G2424

Trust

Every Word of Your's our Deity El the Almighty[a] is pure: You are a shield unto them that put their trust in You.[1] I trust in You the Self Existent Eternal Jehovah[b], and do good; so shalt I dwell in the land, and verily I shalt be fed.[2] But let all those that put their trust in You rejoice: let them ever shout for joy, because You defend them: let them also that love Your name be joyful in You.[3]

Show Your marvelous loving kindness, O You that saves me by Your right hand because I put my trust in You from those that rise up against me.[4] O my Eloheem[c], I trust in You: let me not be ashamed, let not mine enemies triumph over me.[5] You the Self Existent Eternal Jehovah[d] also will be a refuge if I am oppressed, a refuge in times of trouble.[6] And because I know Your name I will put my trust in You: for

You, the Self Existent Eternal Jehovah[e], have not forsaken me because I seek You.[7]

My fathers trusted in You: they trusted, and You did deliver them.[8] They cried unto You, and were delivered: they trusted in You, and were not confounded.[9] So in You, O Self Existent Eternal Jehovah[f], do I put my trust: let me never be put to confusion.[10] I trust in You the Self Existent Eternal Jehovah[g] forever: for in You Yaw the Lord most Vehement[h], the Self Existent Eternal Jehovah[i], is everlasting strength:[11] I trust in You at all times; I am one of Your people, I pour out my heart before You: You Eloheem[j] are a refuge for me. Selah.[12]

You wilt keep me in perfect peace, because my mind is stayed on You : because I trust in You.[13] O LORD of hosts, blessed am I because I trust in You.[14] I cover and seal this prayer with the *Blood of Jesus. In His Name Amen.*

Scripture References

1.	Prov 30:5 KJV	8.	Ps 22:4 KJV
2.	Ps 37:3 KJV	9.	Ps 22:5 KJV
3.	Ps 5:11 KJV	10.	Ps 71:1 KJV
4.	Ps 17:7 KJV	11.	Isa 26:4 KJV
5.	Ps 25:2 KJV	12.	Ps 62:8 KJV
6.	Ps 9:9 KJV	13.	Isa 26:3 KJV
7.	Ps 9:10 KJV	14.	Ps 84:12 KJV

Strong's and Thayer's References

a.	Prov30:5 H433-410	g.	Isa 26:4 H3068
b.	Ps 37:3 H3068	h.	Isa 26:4 H3050
c.	Ps 25:2 H430	i.	Isa 26:4 H3068
d.	Ps 9:9 H3068	j.	Ps 62:8 H430
e.	Ps 9:10 H3068	k.	Ps 84:12 H3068
f.	Ps 71:1 H3068		

Prayer for Unbelief

It is written Jesus my Jehovah Who is Salvation[a] told him, If you can believe, all things are possible to him who believes[1]. So I choose to believe Jesus, to be able to believe that everything is possible for me, because I believe. And like my brothers, I take care that there is not by chance in me an evil heart without belief, turning away from You the living Theos Godhead[b].[2]

With tears flowing, the child's father at once cried out, "I do believe! Help my unbelief!" And so just like the child's father I cry out to You I do believe! Help my unbelief![3] For what? if I have not believed, shall my unbelief make the faith of You the Theos Godhead[c] without effect?[4] No because You El the Almighty[d] are not a man, that You should lie; neither the son of man, that You should repent You do what You say and make good on Your Word.[5]

So I thank You Heavenly Father that You are able to help my unbelief turn into belief. Now unto You the King eternal, immortal, invisible, the only wise Theos Godhead[e], *be honor and glory for ever and ever. Amen.*[6] *I cover and seal this prayer with the Blood of Jesus. In His Name Amen.*

Scripture References

1.   Mark 9:23 WEB
2.   Heb 3:12 BBE
3.   Mark 9:24 WEB
4.   Rom 3:3 KJV
5.   Num 23:19 KJV
6.   1Tim 1:17 KJV

Strong's and Thayer's References

a.   Mark 9:23 G2424
b.   Heb 3:9 G2316
c.   Rom 3:3 G2316
d.   Num 23:19 H410
e.   1 Tim 1:17 G2316

Understanding Eyes to See and Ears to Hear

Father in Heaven it is written that the hearing ear, and the seeing eye, You the Self Existent Eternal Jehovah[a] have made even both of them.[1] Hear, you deaf; and look, you blind, that you may see.[2] For seeing many things, but you observe not; opening the ears, but you hear not.[3]

So I ask that I will look and see and hear and listen. And in that day shall the deaf hear the words of the book, and the eyes of the blind shall see out of obscurity, and out of darkness.[4]

Open my eyes, that I may behold wondrous things out of Your law.[5] I have ears to hear, let me hear.[6] I am one who has ears to hear, let me hear.[7] That You Theos the Godhead Trinity[b] of my Kurios the Master[c], Jesus Christos, the Anointed

Messiah[d], the Father of glory, may give to me the spirit of wisdom and revelation in the knowledge of You:[8]

The eyes of my understanding being enlightened; that I may know what is the hope of Your calling, and what the riches of the glory of Your inheritance in the saints,[9] For there is nothing hid, which shall not be manifested; neither was anything kept secret, but that it should come abroad.[10] I am one who has ears to hear, let me hear.[11]

And Jesus said unto them, Take heed what I hear: with what measure I mete, it shall be measured to me: and unto me that hears shall more be given.[12] For to me who has, to me shall be given: and he that has not, from him shall be taken even that which he has.[13]

Then shall the righteous shine forth as the sun in the kingdom of their Father. Who hath ears to hear, let him hear.[14] *I have ears to hear, let me hear.*[15] *Blessed are my eyes for they see: and my ears, for they hear.*[15] *I cover and seal this prayer with the Blood of Jesus. In His Name Amen.*

Scripture References

1.	Prov 20:12 KJV	9.	Eph 1:18 KJV
2.	Isa 42:18 KJV	10.	Mark 4:22 KJV
3.	Isa 42:20 KJV	11.	Mark 4:23 KJV
4.	Isa 29:18 KJV	12.	Mark 4:24 KJV
5.	Ps 119:18 KJV	13.	Mark 4:25 KJV
6.	Matt 13:9 KJV	14.	Matt 13:43 KJV
7.	Mark 4:23 KJV	15.	Matt 11:15 KJV
8.	Eph 1:17 KJV	16.	Matt 13:16 KJV

Strong's and Thayer's Reference's

a.	Prov 20:12 H3068	c.	Eph 1:7 G2962
b.	Eph 1:17 G2316	d.	Eph 1:7 G5547

Prayer for Waiting on the Lord

O Jehovah the Self Existent One[a], have mercy on me; for I have been waiting for Your help: be my strength every morning, my salvation in time of trouble.[1] I am waiting for You Jehovah the Self Existent One[b], my soul is waiting for You, and my hope is in Your Word.[2] It is good to go on hoping and quietly waiting for the salvation of You Jehovah the Self Existent One[c].[3]

My soul, waits in silence for You Eloheem[d] alone, for my expectation is from You.[4] My soul waits for You Jehovah the Self Existent One[e]: You are my help and my shield.[5] Wait on You Jehovah the Self Existent One[f]: be of good courage, and You shall strengthen my heart: wait, I say, on You Jehovah the Self Existent One[g].[6]

Let integrity and uprightness preserve me, for I wait for You.[7] I have been waiting for Your salvation, O Jehovah the Self Existent One[h].[8] Jehovah the Self Existent One[i] are good to me who is waiting for You, to my soul which is looking for You.[9] Therefore I will look unto You Jehovah the Self Existent One[j]; I will wait for You Eloheem[k] of my salvation: my Eloheem[l] will hear me.[10]

And in that day it will be said, See, You are my Eloheem[m]; I have been waiting for You, and You will be my Saviour: You are Jehovah the Self Existent One[n] in whom is my hope; I will be glad and have delight in Your salvation.[11] I wait patiently for You Jehovah the Self Existent One[o]; and You incline unto me, and hear my cry.[12] I cover and seal this prayer with the Blood of Jesus. In His Name Amen.

Scripture References

1.	Isa 33:2 BBE	5.	Ps 33:20 KJV
2.	Ps 130:5 BBE	6.	Ps 27:14 KJV
3.	Lam 3:26 BBE	7.	Ps 25:21 WEB
4.	Ps 62:5 WEB	8.	Gen 49:18 BBE

9. Lam 3:25 BBE
10. Mic 7:7 KJV

11. Isa 25:9 BBE
12. Ps 40:1 KJV

Strong's and Thayer's References

a. Isa 33:2 H3068
b. Ps 130:5 H3068
c. Lam 3:26 H3068
d. Ps 62:5 H430
e. Ps 33:20 H3068
f. Ps 27:14 H3068
g. Ps 27:14 H3068
h. Gen 49:18 H3068

i. Lam 3:25 H3068
j. Mic 7:7 H3068
k. Mic 7:7 H430
l. Mic 7:7 H430
m. Isa 25:9 H430
n. Isa 25:9 H3068
o. Ps 40:1 H3056

Prayer When Slandered

Heavenly Father it is written blessed am I, when men shall revile me, and persecute me, and shall say all manner of evil against me falsely, for Your sake.[1] I rejoice, and be exceeding glad: for great is my reward in heaven: for so persecuted they the prophets which were before me.[2]

You shall send from heaven, and save me from the reproach of him that would swallow me up. Selah. You Eloheem[a] shall send forth Your mercy and Your truth.[3] I Hearken unto You, and know righteousness, I am a person in whose heart is Your law; I fear not the reproach of men, neither am afraid of their revilings.[4] If I be reproached for the name of You the Anointed Messiah[b], happy am I; for the spirit of glory and You Theos the Godhead Trinity[c] rests upon me: on their part You are evil spoken of, but on my part You are glorified.⁵

For I have heard the slander of many: fear was on every side: while they took counsel together against me, they devised to take away my life.⁶ But I trust in You, O Self Existent Eternal Jehovahᵈ: I said, You are my Eloheemᵉ.⁷ My times are in Your hand: deliver me from the hand of my enemies, and from them that persecute me.⁸ Make Your face to shine upon me Your servant: save me for Your mercies sake.⁹

Let me not be ashamed, O Self Existent Eternal Jehovahᶠ; for I have called upon thee: let the wicked be ashamed, and let them be silent in the grave.¹⁰ Let the lying lips be put to silence; which speak grievous things proudly and contemptuously against the righteous.¹¹ Oh how great is Your goodness, which You have laid up for me that fears You; which

You have wrought for me that trust in You before the sons of men!*12*

You shall hide me in the secret of Your presence from the pride of man: You shall keep me secretly in a pavilion from the strife of tongues.*13* Blessed be You the Self Existent Eternal Jehovah*g*: for You have showed me Your marvelous kindness in a strong city.*14* I cover and seal this prayer with the Blood of Jesus. In His Name Amen.

Scripture References

1. Matt 5:11 KJV
2. Matt 5:12 KJV
3. Ps 57:3 KJV
4. Isa 51:7 KJV
5. 1Pet 4:14 KJV
6. Ps 31:13 KJV
7. Ps 31:14 KJV
8. Ps 31:15 KJV
9. Ps 31:16 KJV
10. Ps 31:17 KJV
11. Ps 31:18 KJV
12. Ps 31:19 KJV
13. Ps 31:20 KJV
14. Ps 31:21 KJV

Strong's and Thayer's References

a. Ps 57:3 H430
b. 1Pet 4:14 G5547
c. 1Pet 4:14 G2316
d. Ps 31:14 H3068
e. Ps 31:14 H430
f. Ps 31:17 H3068
g. Ps 31:21 H3068

Prayer for Wisdom

Heavenly Father it is written If any of you lack wisdom, let him ask of You Theos the Godhead Trinity[a] , because You give to all men liberally, and upbraid not; and it shall be given him.[1] But let him ask in faith, nothing wavering. For he that wavers is like a wave of the sea driven with the wind and tossed.[2] So I ask in faith for wisdom and I believe by faith that You give it to me.

For You the Self Existent Eternal Jehovah[b] give wisdom: out of Your mouth comes knowledge and understanding.[3] You lay up sound wisdom for the righteous: You are a buckler to them that walk uprightly.[4] You say get wisdom, get understanding: forget it not; neither decline from the words of Your mouth.[5] Forsake her not, and she shall preserve thee: love her, and she shall keep thee.[6]

Wisdom is the principal thing; therefore get wisdom: and with all our getting get understanding.[7] I want to know wisdom and instruction; to perceive the words of understanding;[8] So that my ear will listen to wisdom, and apply my heart to understanding.[9] I get wisdom, get understanding: forget it not; neither decline from the Words of Your mouth.[10] I will not forsake her, and she shall preserve me: I will love her, and she shall keep me.[11] Wisdom is the principal thing; therefore get wisdom: and with all my getting get understanding.[12]

Happy is the man that finds wisdom, and the man that gets understanding.[13] So let me find wisdom and get understanding. You say my son, let not them depart from your eyes: keep sound wisdom and *discretion:*[14] *So shall they be life unto my soul, and grace to thy neck.*[15]

For You will give me a mouth and wisdom, which all my adversaries shall not be able to gainsay nor resist.[16] *And they will not be able to resist the wisdom and the spirit by which I speak.*[17] *For wisdom is better than rubies; and all the things that may be desired are not to be compared to it.*[18] *I thank You for wisdom Abba. I cover and seal this prayer with the Blood of Jesus. In His Name Amen.*

Scripture References

1.	Jas 1:5 KJV	10.	Prov 4:5 KJV
2.	Jas 1:6 KJV	11.	Prov 4:6 KJV
3.	Prov 2:6 KJV	12.	Prov 4:7 KJV
4.	Prov 2:7 KJV	13.	Prov 3:13 KJV
5.	Prov 4:5 KJV	14.	Prov 3:21 KJV
6.	Prov 4:6 KJV	15.	Prov 3:22 KJV
7.	Prov 4:7 KJV	16.	Luke 21:15 KJV
8.	Prov 1:2 KJV	17.	Acts 6:10 KJV
9.	Prov 2:2 KJV	18.	Prov 8:11 KJV

Strong's and Thayer's References

a.	Jas 1:5 G2316	b.	Prov 2:6 H3068

You Were Created on Purpose

You Eloheem[a] created man in Your own image, in the image of You Eloheem[b] , You created him; male and female You created them.[1] From the beginning of the creation You Theos the Godhead trinity made us male and female.[2] And You Eloheem[d] saw everything that You had made, and, behold, it was very good. And the evening and the morning were the sixth day.[3]

You say that You the Self Existent Eternal Jehovah[e], are my redeemer, and You that formed me from the womb, You are the Self Existent Eternal Jehovah[f] that makes all things; that stretches forth the heavens alone; that spreads abroad the earth by Yourself;[4] You the Self Existent Eternal Jehovah[g] are Eloheem[h]: it is You that has made me, and not me myself; I am one of

160

Your people, and a sheep of Your pasture.[5]

You the Self Existent Eternal Jehovah[i] will perfect that which concerns me: Your mercy, O Self Existent Eternal Jehovah[j], endures forever: forsake not the works of Your own hands.[6]

Did You not make others as well as me? did You not give us life in our mothers' bodies? As I know not what is the way of the spirit, or how the bones do grow in the womb of her that is with child: even so I know not the works of You Eloheem[k] who makes all.[8] For You formed my inmost being. You knit me together in my mother's womb.[9] I will give thanks to You, for I am fearfully and wonderfully made. Your works are wonderful, my soul knows that very well.[10] My frame wasn't hidden from You, when I was made in secret, woven together in the depths of the earth.[11] Your eyes saw my body.

 In your book they were all written, the days that were ordained for me, when as yet there were none of them.[12] How precious also are thy thoughts unto me, O El the Almighty[l]! how great is the sum of them! If I would count them, they are more in number than the sand. When I wake up, I am still with You.[14] Many, O Self Existent Eternal Jehovah[m] my Eloheem[n], are Your wonderful works which You have done, and Your thoughts which are to me: they cannot be reckoned up in order unto You: if I would declare and speak of them, they are more than can be numbered.[15]

For You know the thoughts that You think toward me, says You the Self Existent Eternal Jehovah[o], thoughts of peace, and not of evil, to give me an expected future[p].[16] The Spirit of

162

You El the Almighty[q] has made me, and the breath of You the Almighty has given me life.[17] I cover and seal this prayer with the Blood of Jesus. In His Name Amen.

Scripture References

1.	Gen 1:27 KJV	10.	Ps 139:14 WEB
2.	Mark 10:6 KJV	11.	Ps 139:15 WEB
3.	Gen 1:31 KJV	12.	Ps 139:16 WEB
4.	Isa 44:24 KJV	13.	Ps 139:17 WEB
5.	Ps 100:3 KJV	14.	Ps 139:18 WEB
6.	Ps 138:8 KJV	15.	Ps 40:5 KJV
7.	Job 31:15 BBE	16.	Jer 29:11 KJV
8.	Eccl 11:5 KJV	17.	Job 33:4 KJV
9.	Ps 139:13 WEB		

Strong's and Thayer's References

a.	Gen 1:27 H430	j.	Ps 138:8 H3068
b.	Gen 1:27 H430	k.	Eccl 11:5 H430
c.	Mark 10:6 G2316	l.	Ps 139:17 H410
d.	Gen 1:31 H430	m.	Ps 40:5 H3068
e.	Isa 44:24 H3068	n.	Ps 40:5 H430
f.	Isa 44:24 H3068	o.	Jer 29:11 H3068
g.	Ps 100:3 H3068	p.	Jer 29:11 H319
h.	Ps 100:3 H430	q.	Job 33:4 H410
i.	Ps 138:8 H3068		

Prayer for Your Calling

Heavenly Father You who have saved me, and called me with a holy calling, not according to my works, but according to Your own purpose and grace, which was given me in the anointed Messiah[a] Jesus before the world began,[1] That I might walk worthy of You Kurios the Master[b] unto all pleasing, being fruitful in every good work, and increasing in the knowledge of You Theos the Godhead Trinity[c2]

Being strengthened with all might, according to Your glorious power, unto all patience and longsuffering with joyfulness.[3]

And I know that all things work together for good to me because I love You Theos the Godhead Trinity[d], and am called according to Your purpose.[4]

For me who You did foreknow, You also did predestinate to be conformed to the image of Your Son, that He might be the firstborn among many brethren.[5] Moreover me who You did predestinate, me You also called: and me who You called, You also justified: and me who You justified, me You also glorified.[6]

That You would grant to me, that I being delivered out of the hand of my enemies might serve You without fear,[7] In holiness and righteousness before You, all the days of my life[8] And whatsoever I do, to do it heartily, as to You Kurios the Master[e], and not unto men;[9] I press toward the mark for the prize of the high calling of You Theos the Godhead Trinity in the anointed Messiah Jesus[g].[10] I cover and seal this prayer with the Blood of Jesus. In His Name Amen.

Scripture References

1.	2Tim 1:9 KJV	6.	Rom 8:30 KJV
2.	Col 1:10 KJV	7.	Luke 1:74 KJV
3.	Col 1:11 KJV	8.	Luke 1:75 KJV
4.	Rom 8:28 KJV	9.	Col 3:23 KJV
5.	Rom 8:29 KJV	10.	Phil 3:14 KJV

Strong's and Thayer's References

a.	2 Tim 1:9 G5547	e.	Col 3:23 G2962
b.	Col 1:10 G2962	f.	Phil 3:14 G2316
c.	Col 1:10 G2316	g.	Phil 3:14 G5547
d.	Rom 8:28 G2316		

Abbreviations Superscript & Subscripts Chart

Superscript & Subscripts references are found after the preceding scriptures and names in all the prayers.

Gen	Genesis
Exod	Exodus
Lev	Leviticus
Num	Numbers
Deut	Deuteronomy
Josh	Joshua
Judg	Judges
Ruth	Ruth
1Sam	1 Samuel
2Sam	2 Samuel
1Kgs	1 Kings
2Kgs	2 Kings
1Chr	1 Chronicles
2Chr	2 Chronicles
Ezra	Ezra
Neh	Nehemiah
Esth	Esther
Job	Job
Ps	Psalms
Prov	Proverbs
Eccl	Ecclesiastes
Song	Song of Solomon
Isa	Isaiah
Jer	Jeremiah
Lam	Lamentations
Ezek	Ezekiel
Dan	Daniel
Hos	Hosea
Joel	Joel

Amos	Amos
Obad	Obadiah
Jonah	Jonah
Mic	Micah
Nah	Nahum
Hab	Habakkuk
Zeph	Zephaniah
Hag	Haggai
Zech	Zechariah
Mal	Malachi
Matt	Matthew
Mark	Mark
Luke	Luke
John	John
Acts	Acts
Rom	Romans
1Cor	1 Corinthians
2Cor	2 Corinthians
Gal	Galatians
Eph	Ephesians
Phil	Philippians
Col	Colossians
1Thess	1 Thessalonians
2Thess	2 Thessalonians
1Tim	1 Timothy
2Tim	2 Timothy
Titus	Titus
Phlm	Philemon
Heb	Hebrews
Jas	James
1Pet	1 Peter
2Pet	2 Peter
1John	1 John
2John	2 John

3John	3 John
Jude	Jude
Rev	Revelation
S	Strong's Hebrew
G	Thayer's Greek
Superscript Numbers [7]	Scripture References
Subscript Alphabet w	Dictionary References
KJV	King James Bible
BBE	Bible in Basic English
WEB	World English Bible

Author

I Love the Lord with all my spirit, soul and body and have submitted all to Him. The fruit of this has enabled me to enjoy a transparent relationship with my Abba Daddy and my Ishi. I am my beloved's, and my beloved is mine....Song of Solomon 6:3

I have a passion for His Word and have been writing scripture prayers since 1998. Ongoing enrollment with the school of the Holy Ghost provides an interesting journey which has included many tests, and assignments. A few tests I had to do over, Ouch ! During the times in the fire the Lord and His Word has been my source of truth and encouragement.

His Word is settled in heaven, Psalm 119:89 and is settled in my heart too.

Kim Eisnor

More Books

www.ingramcontent.com/pod-product-compliance
Lightning Source LLC
La Vergne TN
LVHW051631080426
835511LV00016B/2298